PENGUIN HANDBOOKS

PENGUIN LIVING CRAFTS
General Editor: Walter Brooks

Down to Earth

Wes Gorham was born in Westport, Connecticut, in 1908. He received his D.O. degree from the Philadelphia College of Osteopathic Medicine in 1931 and went on to do graduate study in New York. In 1933 he established practice in Norwalk, Connecticut, where he specializes in industrial medicine and X-ray diagnosis. Dr. Gorham first experienced the joys of gardening at the age of five, when he spent a number of weeks with his maternal grandparents at their old farmhouse in the apple-producing countryside of southwestern Connecticut. His grandfather staked off a small garden plot of a few square yards, explaining it was to be his own little garden that he was to plant and care for. The author relates that nothing during his childhood was comparable to the joy of that little garden and the puzzlement of how those tiny seeds grew into so many different vegetables and flowers. In his late thirties he gradually experienced a strong impulse to return to the soil, and it wasn't long before he had a large collection of national prizewinning hybrid irises. When Dr. Gorham subsequently sustained a severe back injury, he turned to indoor gardening. A period of research and experimentation followed which taught him that indoor gardening is an exacting discipline that may be reduced to a small number of basic fundamentals.These make the difference between success and failure.

WES GORHAM

Down To Earth

A Guide to Successful Indoor Gardening

Illustrated by
Walter Brooks

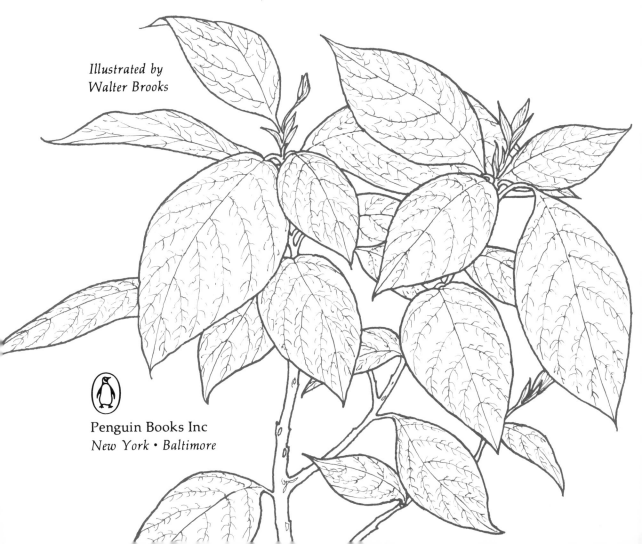

Penguin Books Inc
New York • Baltimore

Penguin Books Inc
72 Fifth Avenue
New York, New York 10011

Penguin Books Inc
7110 Ambassador Road
Baltimore, Maryland 21207

First published 1974
Reprinted 1975

Preface

The myth of the proverbial green thumb must be considered an unreliable old wives' tale. Proficiency in gardening comes not from some mystical natural endowment but from a working knowledge of the basic requirements of all plant life.

It is indeed fortunate that most houseplants have an inherent capacity to adjust to reasonable environmental changes and that the attention they do require is meager compared to the joy, satisfaction, and pleasure they afford the discerning indoor gardener.

The purpose of this book is to provide the indoor gardener with a select list of dependable and virtually care-free houseplants that can be grown successfully with minimal effort in one's house or apartment. The number of plants presented has been intentionally restricted to allow a more comprehensive dissertation of the culture of each. Unless specified to the contrary, these plants are nondemanding and not overly temperamental.

All plants need light, warmth, water, soil, nourishment, and protection from their natural enemies. The control of these fundamental requisites is the key to successful indoor floriculture and the secret of the professional floriculturist. "The difference between failure and success is doing a thing nearly right and doing it exactly right"—Edward C. Simmons.

W. G.

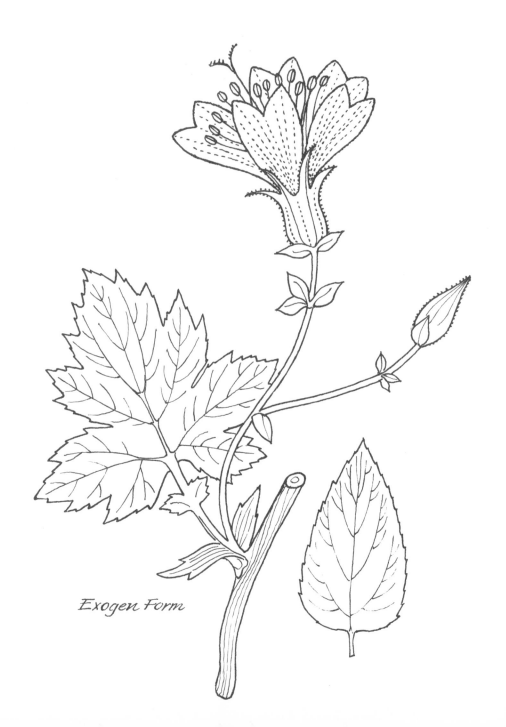

Exogen Form

Contents

SECTION THREE
Plants for Foliage

SECTION FOUR

Succulent Plants

APPENDIXES

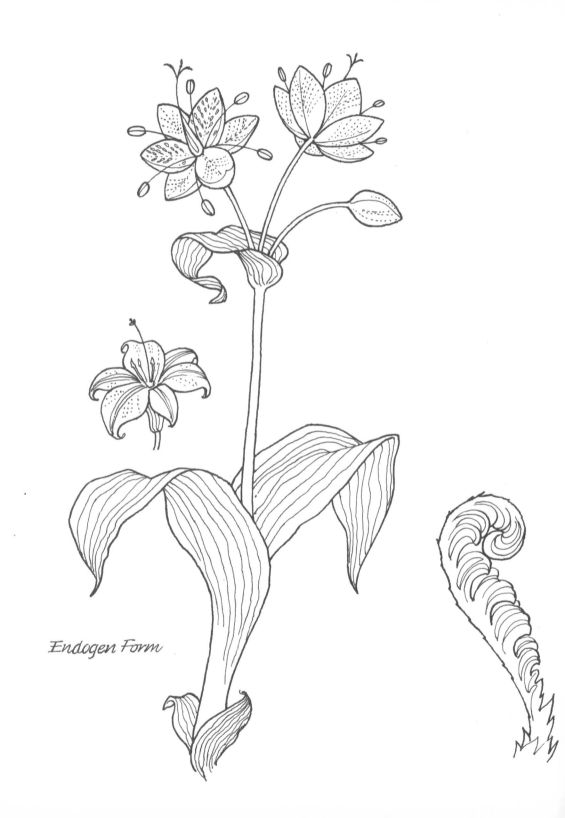

Endogen Form

Fundamentals for Successful Floriculture

What a desolate place would be a world without flowers?—It would be a face without a smile; a feast without a welcome—Are not flowers the stars of the earth?—And are not our stars the flowers of heaven?

—Mrs. Balfour (1808–1878)

Fern Form

Light

Light is the most important basic requirement for the successful cultivation of houseplants. A plant placed in an environment devoid of light shortly loses its freshness and vigor and eventually withers and dies. Both sunlight and artificial light are forms of luminous energy that travel approximately 186,300 miles per second, and both are visible. A plant exposed to light is able by means of certain complicated biochemical conversions to manufacture its food for sustenance, vigor, and growth.

Sunlight is composed of a vast number of invisible rays, two of which are of importance to the indoor garden: ultraviolet rays and infrared rays. Human beings, when exposed to ultraviolet radiation in excess, suffer sunburn. Likewise, ultraviolet radiation can have a deleterious effect upon plant life and if prolonged and intense, has the capacity to cause total plant destruction. Man senses the presence of infrared rays by the comforting sensation of warmth. Plant life requires and absorbs this type of solar energy for growth.

We have no need to become entangled in the vast maze of scientific knowledge and terminology concerning light and plant life. The terms *chlorophyll* and *photosynthesis* are, however, of the utmost importance. These two words cut through the prodigious amount of scientific jargon and for all practical purposes, suffice to explain the miraculous effect of light upon plant life.

In review:

Chlorophyll is the green coloring substance found in the earth's vegetation.

Photosynthesis is the biochemical process by which a plant is able to manufacture sugar and starch for its nourishment, through the effect of sunlight acting upon its chlorophyll.

At first these definitions will probably appear overly elementary and of little consequence in these involved modern times. How wrong such a first impression would be, for within these definitions will be found the very key of life. The awesome fact is that if all the precious chlorophyll in the world were suddenly destroyed by some catastrophic disaster of global proportion, photosynthesis could no longer take place, and all plant life on earth would cease to exist. This world would

13

then be without food and very shortly thereafter without man, animal, fish, or fowl, and our planet would suddenly become as naked and desolate as the moon.

People in general are aware of the necessity and benefits of sleep and rest, yet few realize that members of the vegetable kingdom are also living organisms and that they, too, require hours of rest. Like man, when the day's work is over and the hours of darkness have arrived, our plants enter a cyclic state of rest, which continues until the next daybreak.

It has been ascertained by comprehensive research that plants vary in regard to the number of hours of light they require and the number of hours of rest they need. Excellent texts that cover this topic in depth can be obtained by those desirous of delving further into this vital and interesting subject.

Mother Nature has favored the amateur gardener with good fortune, for it has been discovered that most plants do well with twelve to fourteen hours of light, and I call them flexible plants because of their gratifying adaptability.

As we have discussed light, its components, effects, and importance, let us now consider the light sources available in an average home. There are two general sources; sunlight and artificial light. Many plants thrive behind a sunny window with a southern exposure. Others prefer the partial sunlight of an east or a west window. Lastly, there is a group of plants that require little more than the constant but low-level illumination from the north.

The artificial light employed by indoor gardeners is obtained through the use of the incandescent lamp or the fluorescent lamp. Artificial lighting is commonly used to compensate for the lack of light beyond the hours of sundown or during dismal, sunless days. Plants, however, must not be exposed to artificial light overnight, for the price of over-work and insufficient rest is the same with plants as it is with people.

Many plants are grown exclusively under fluorescent lamps manufactured especially for the indoor gardener's use and for professional research. I personally favor the Gro-Lux lamps manufactured by the Sylvania Lighting Products Company, which impart a pleasing purplish-violet color to plants. It is popular to mix incandescent and fluorescent lighting. I recommend, however, that the novice indoor gardener confine his artificial lighting to the fluorescent lamp.

For those who must garden with limited house space, modern technology makes fluorescent indoor gardening not only possible but also

decorative by adding living beauty to the decor of one's home. Special floriculture fluorescent fixtures are obtainable at most local garden centers, and many manufacturers sell directly to consumers. These fixtures are made in many shapes and sizes and are available in numerous decorative colors and designs.

Specific light requirements for individual plants are dealt with in Sections Two, Three, and Four of this book.

Warmth

The control of the environmental temperature within the immediate proximity of houseplants is of the utmost importance. The effects of controlled heat upon plants might be compared to baking powder in the making of a cake, both acting as catalytic agents. The process of photosynthesis cannot take place without warmth; thus temperature is vital in floriculture.

Research has established that a variation of temperatures during day and night hours is essential. Most houseplants prove their ability to

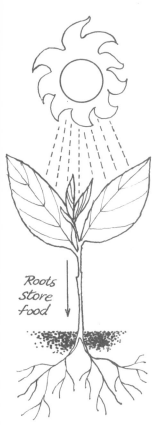

Roots
store
food

adapt to reasonable environmental temperature changes such as a daytime temperature range of 60° F. to 75° F. and a night temperature as low as 50° F. Designations such as "cool" and "warm" plants may be employed as a guide for proper temperature control. Fortunately, most houseplants fit one or the other of these categories and display their preference by vigorous growth when placed in the environmental temperature of their liking. In general, the night temperature should be approximately 10° lower than the day temperature. The ideal day and night temperature for each select plant is presented in Sections Two, Three, and Four of this book.

Before concluding our consideration of the importance of temperature control, let us review the physiological processes that take place in a plant during the cooler hours of darkness. Plants work feverishly during the hours of daylight producing and storing food, but they cease this labor upon the advent of darkness and enter a period of rest, during which time they assimilate their stored food and grow. A drop in temperature at night is vital to this botanical physiology.

Nature wisely provides a variation between day and night temperatures, first with the heat of the sun during the day and then with a refreshing drop in temperature upon the first appearance of the cooling shadows of dusk. When we take plants indoors, we must provide a similar temperature variation.

Ventilation

The practice of providing fresh air to replace accumulated stale air is one worthy of adoption. Ventilation helps a plant to exhale or transpire through its leaves, which is the method by which plants dispose of waste products. It aids a plant in disease control and, as well, prevents the formation of disastrous concentrations of noxious fumes such as manufactured cooking gas and automobile combustion fumes. Above all, ventilation furnishes a fresh supply of life-supporting oxygen and other atmospheric gases vital in plant-life physiology.

Whatever method of ventilation is employed, one must guard against direct drafts, which have an adverse effect upon houseplants in general.

Besides frequent airing of your plants, an axiom worthy of remembering is: Never crowd your plants, for it is wiser to have fewer plants, with more room for air to circulate, than to have many compressed, inhibited, air-hungry weaklings on your hands.

Water

Every houseplant enthusiast knows the importance of water for plant-life survival; many, however, are not aware of its exact role in plant physiology. Water acts as the vehicle of transportation and the means of rendering many organic and inorganic substances botanically assimilable.

A plant, be it a dwarf or a giant, is a living complex organism with a fascinating anatomy and a wondrous physiology. It is a biochemical production factory capable of converting many of the earth's elements and compounds into food and energy for growth and propagation. The life-sustaining circulation that serves to transport these raw materials to areas of conversion and storage could not function without water. Transpiration, the process by which a plant disposes of its waste products, could not take place, either, if water were not present to carry these waste materials to the plant's leaves for disposal.

The role of water is therefore much more complex than just keeping a plant's soil moist and its roots cool. The plant not only relies on water for its life process but also relies on you to replace the water it consumes and the water it throws off during transpiration. Wild plants must adjust to nature's capriciousness or die; houseplants, hopefully, can expect to be protected from dehydration or drowning when they are taken into an artificial environment. This is the "why" of watering. The "when," the "how," and the "how much" must also be considered.

Arbitrary watering schedules that purport to apply to any collection of plants, regardless of species, are meant to be helpful but in reality are superficial and dangerous. Directions such as "water daily" or "water weekly" have a sensible basis only when the needs of a particular plant are known. All plants can be divided into three categories. As with their human counterparts, there are the light drinkers, the moderate drinkers, and the heavy drinkers. Once these distinctions are established, a general schedule for watering can be worked out. Beyond this, water retention and consumption will vary according to the type of soil used, the size of the pot, the indoor climate, and, of course, whether the plant is actively growing, blooming, or dormant.

The most water-loving plant can literally be drowned, and even the most conservative of the water-consumers can suffer dehydration. It is not daily watering that is the ideal but rather daily observation of the plant's soil condition and overall well-being. Touching the surface of the soil is the best way to determine whether water is needed. Most plants like a moderately moist soil, and watering programs can be geared to both the plant's needs and the indoor gardener's convenience. There are even alternatives to hand watering that allow for periods of time when the plants must be left unattended.

I water the majority of my plants from the top, using water at room temperature. It is important to keep saucers under all pots and to discard any water that drains from the pots into the saucers. Many plants enjoy periodic sink soakings, which is accomplished by placing the pots in a deep sink and bringing the water level just up to the brim of the pots. The duration of these soaking sessions is determined by the specific requirements of the plant, the size of the pot, and the characteristics of the potting soil. After the plants have been removed and allowed to drain, saucers should be emptied.

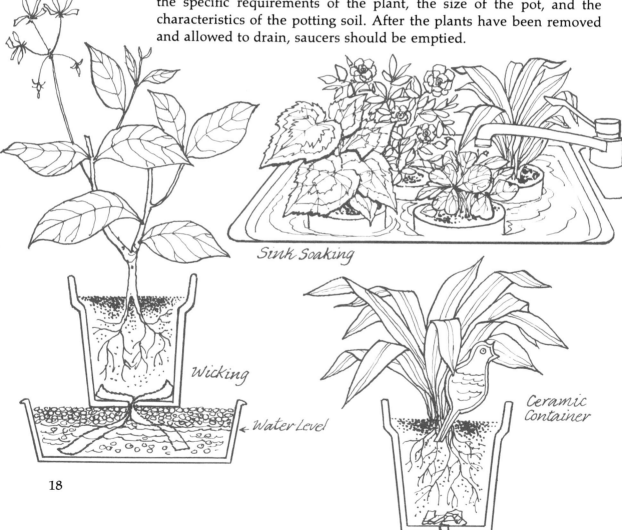

Sink Soaking

Wicking

← Water Level

Ceramic Container

Plants can be watered from the bottom by setting them in trays about three inches deep with a layer of pebbles. Water is added to one inch or so above the pebbles, and the plants are allowed to remain until the surface of the soil is moist to the touch. Wicking is another method of bottom watering. A wick such as those sold in garden centers can be placed in the pot before the soil and the plant are added. This wick is positioned so that it protrudes from the bottom of the pot. The plant is then placed on a bed of pebbles in a tray of water, with the wick inserted in the water below. Capillary attraction draws water up into the soil.

Small ceramic water containers with narrow tubes for insertion into the soil of the pot are available in stores. These release water slowly over a period of time and are useful when plants must be left alone for a few days. Wicking is also a satisfactory method of providing water when plants are temporarily unattended.

Sections Two, Three, and Four, which describe plants for flowering, plants for foliage, and succulent plants, include specific watering instructions.

Humidity

A close friend who is a heating and air-conditioning expert claims that the average house or apartment, in regions requiring seasonal heating, may become as dry as the Sahara Desert. This fact is important in the practice of plant care, for the drier the environmental atmosphere, the faster and greater the plant's water loss. This brings us to the subject of humidity, which is the amount of water vapor in the air. More often, you will hear the term "relative humidity," which, briefly, means the moisture content of the air expressed as a percentage of the total amount the air could hold at that particular temperature. Assuming a heated apartment to have an average temperature of 68° F. to 72° F., the relative humidity would generally be about 20 percent. Any indoor environment in which man is comfortable will, with certain adjustments, satisfy the majority of houseplants. At extremely low humidity levels, when man is prone to complain of a dry throat and parched nasal passages, plants also suffer. They display the injurious effects by generalized wilting, leaf dropping, and withering.

Most plants do prefer a much more humid atmosphere than man, but the latter would experience discomfort and also chagrin at dripping walls; therefore, a compromise must be found. With assistance, plants

19

Mister

←Pebbles
← Water

will adapt, and coexistence is possible.

Obviously, if we make our homes comfortable for ourselves, we are also accommodating most of our plants, but what of those that need more moisture than we care to put into our environment through adjustments or supplements to heating equipment?

A few time-tested practices have been developed over the years to raise overly low levels of relative humidity. When one is without modern expensive equipment, he may employ these practices. He will find daily watering and foliage mist sprayings twice a day helpful. He can purchase or make a receptacle or tray of metal, plastic, or fiber glass (at least three inches deep) to use as a planter humidifier. This is done by filling the tray with two inches of gravel, pebbles, or sand and by adding sufficient water to create a water level just below the top of the fill. The water will evaporate into the atmosphere, aiding considerably to raise the relative humidity in the immediate area. The indoor gardener may favor a plant by taking it into his bathroom while he showers. He might recall his grandmother boiling water and explaining, "I'm making steam for my plants." He might also greatly benefit his plants by using water vapor but produce it by more modern means, such as an electric croup kettle or vaporizer. Finally, and probably best, he could consider purchasing any one of the moderately priced portable humidifiers, which are quite efficient.

Excessively high relative humidity is less of a problem, as it is usually encountered in the tropics and areas with extended rainy seasons. Fortunately, in most areas periods of high humidity are not prolonged beyond the limits of man's endurance or the lasting powers of plant life.

Soil

In between each houseplant and its pot there must be some kind of soil. This is one aspect on which all indoor gardeners agree. Beyond this, soil mixtures are touted in a myriad of variations, but the ones we choose for consideration originate from two sources: land soil (garden loam or rich earth) and manufactured soil (packaged commercial products in various combinations that may, or may not, contain processed earth).

The principal function of a growing medium is to sustain vegetation or plant life physically and chemically. Physically, it stabilizes a plant,

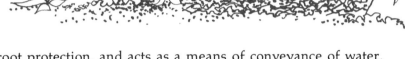

provides root protection, and acts as a means of conveyance of water, nutrients, and air to the roots. Chemically, it supplies certain minerals and nutrients that are botanically assimilable.

It is just as true today as in the past that the most frequently used soil for growing houseplants is obtained from one's garden or land. The average garden surface or topsoil usually requires little modification because of accumulation of rich organic material that develops over the years largely from decomposed vegetation. The necessary and continuous cultivation of one's garden aerates, crumbles, and fluffs the soil by mixing the decomposed organic materials and markedly improves the soil's productivity.

Natural soils must be evaluated to determine if further modification is necessary. In many areas the soil is too alkaline or too acid. It may be heavy and laden with clay or gravel or too sandy. It is imperative that these earth faults be corrected by the addition of one or all of the following substances:

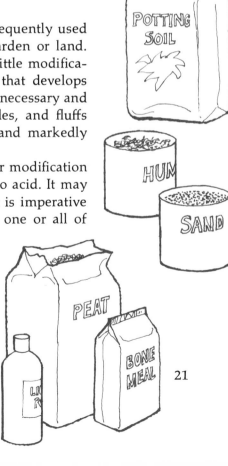

    Loam or rich topsoil
    Builder's sand (sharp sand, not salty sea sand)
    Leaf mold or humus
    Peat moss
    Fertilizer
    Bone meal
    Chemical neutralizers for acid or alkaline soils

21

If potting soil is gathered from outdoors, whether it be a soil mixture or plain garden soil, it should be pasteurized before use. This is accomplished by adding water to it and cooking it in a 180° F. oven for a half hour. Soil pasteurization destroys harmful outdoor microorganisms and other undesirable subterranean life that if brought into your home could result in serious disease and possible destruction of your precious plant collection. It is unfortunate that, at best, soil pasteurization is a messy, malodorous task that the average plant fancier may attempt once but is not apt to repeat a second time.

Many floriculturists employ sterilization rather than pasteurization, a process that renders soil mixtures essentially sterile. This type of soil treatment is performed by the use of chemicals, steam, or electricity. All of these methods, however, are too involved for the average indoor gardener, and further discussion of the subject would not be within the purpose of this book.

For the do-it-yourselfer who is willing to make his own soil mixture, I recommend the following as an ideally balanced potting-soil recipe in which most houseplants will grow and thrive:

2 parts rich garden loam
1 part humus or leaf mold
1 part builder's sand
½ teaspoon commercially prepared fertilizer or bone
    meal for each five- to six-inch pot

As stated earlier, all mixtures that contain outdoor substances should be pasteurized for indoor use. Fertilizer should be added after this process has been completed and the mixture has cooled.

I feel strongly that all homemade potting-soil concoctions, including the one I have just recommended, are a poor substitute for commercial growing mixtures. In addition to the muss, fuss, and bother, there is the difficulty and frustration or trying to find the proper ingredients in this age of urban living.

Throughout this book you will find that I highly recommend commercial growing mixtures produced exclusively for houseplants and obtainable at garden centers and supermarkets. These growing mixtures are manufactured by specialists in the field and, in my opinion, are vastly superior to homemade soil mixtures. In addition, they have a built-in advantage, for they are pasteurized before being packaged.

The amazing modern soilless mixtures meet the important requisites for growing media and are becoming progressively more popular among plant fanciers. There are many excellent brands of soilless mixtures. I use Park's Sure-Fire Gro Mix for my potted plants and Park's Sure-Fire Sowing Mix as a growing medium when starting plants from seed.

The George W. Park Seed Company, Inc., of Greenwood, South Carolina, has extended permission to quote from their attractive and comprehensive catalog, "Park's Flower Book."

The "Sure-Fire" mixes are new growing media composed of equal parts of shredded peat moss and fine-grade Terra-Lite vermiculite, plus nutrients. These are essentially sterile. We now use them for all our plants. If you have a soil problem, these "Sure-Fire" mixes are for you. They were developed by plant scientists at Cornell University and tested throughout the floral industry. Park's "Sure-Fire" Gro Mix assures a balanced diet for your fast-growing plants for up to eight weeks. Gro Mix is the best medium we know of because all plants can be grown successfully with it in any size pot, basket, tub, or greenhouse bench. It eliminates the need to have a special soil recipe for each plant. Gro Mix holds more moisture without waterlogging which means less watering chores for you. Park's "Sure-Fire" Sowing Mix is designed as a growing medium for seeds. We use it for starting the thousands of different varieties for our trial grounds and have excellent results even with unusually hard to grow slow-germinating items. The mix contains just the right amount of necessary nutrients to get the seedlings off to a good start.

The commercially prepared potting media, in general, and the modern soilless mixtures, in particular, are an inestimable boon to those who have limited time and space.

Potting

Until fairly recently when one mentioned a flowerpot, he usually referred to the common red-clay pot. Today, he could be alluding to a ceramic, plastic, Styrofoam, or peat pot, to mention but a few materials currently employed by manufacturers of plant containers. Except for peat pots and those made from other nutrient materials, most containers are inert and merely serve to hold a growing medium.

Proper drainage is of much greater importance than the material from which a container is made. Regardless of the size, shape, beauty, or cost of a plant container, it is harmful if it fails to have an aperture large enough to allow adequate drainage. One would be better off with a discarded coffee can with a few puncture holes in the bottom. Plants must have water, but they will not tolerate constant "wet feet." The principal requisites for proper drainage are as follows: a porous growing medium, an adequate drainage aperture, and a one-inch layer of any inert solid material dropped into the bottom of the pot before filling it. Pieces of crockery from clay or ceramic pots, stones, pebbles, or gravel are ideal for this purpose. Most ornamental plants like gentle confinement and when potted, enjoy being held or supported firmly but not solidly compressed. A plant is ready for a change when its roots are observed growing out of the bottom of its pot. When repotting, it is better not to place a plant in a pot larger than necessary; usually a pot one or two sizes larger is best.

Dirty pots can be a source of plant disease, so all used pots should be thoroughly scrubbed with a detergent and rinsed with boiling water before reuse.

Houseplants that have not outgrown their pots still need a complete change of growing medium every two to two and a half years. This avoids the accumulation of chemicals and corrects the gradual impoverishment that occurs in all potting soils.

one-inch layer

Tap gently
pull pot away

press soil
firmly

Feeding and Nutrients

The material under the headings "Light," "Warmth," "Water," and "Soil" actually covers most of what is essential for feeding, for it is through these that a plant is able to synthesize its food. Making certain that one's plants receive adequate amounts of these basic and essential elements is analogous to feeding them, and therefore they may be considered plant food.

When considering additional plant nourishment, I prefer to think of fertilization rather than feeding, and I liken nutrients to supplementary food products such as vitamins, minerals, and enzymes. Most fertilizers contain the three chemicals that are essential for plant growth, vitality, and well-being. These are: nitrogen (ammonium nitrate) for general plant growth, particularly foliage to which it imparts the deep-green coloring characteristic of healthy plants; phosphorus, which promotes root-system growth, accelerates the maturing process, and encourages budding and blooming; and potassium (potash), which acts as a general plant tonic and is a factor in disease resistance.

Failure to supply these accessory nutrients or chemicals will result in generalized plant debility. If your plant is lacking in nitrogen, the deficiency will result in a progressive loss of foliage coloring, and its leaves will become a pale, sickly, washed-out green or an unforgettable sickly yellow. If a phosphorous deficiency exists, a plant will suffer slow root growth, and the entire plant will be retarded. Potassium deficiency manifests itself by the absence of normal blooming or flowering and drooping of stems and terminal branches.

Most commercial fertilizers designate the nitrogen, phosphorus, and potassium content in percentages. If you see figures such as 4–8–4 or 15–30–15, it will signify that the first preparation contains 4 percent nitrogen, 8 percent phosphorus, and 4 percent potassium, and the second contains 15 percent nitrogen, 30 percent phosphorus, and 15 percent potassium. When added, the three numbers represent the total percentage of available primary plant food. The balance consists of inert substances.

When you next visit a garden center, hardware store, or nursery, locate the fertilizer section and read the labels of several brands. It is a worthwhile practice, and the knowledge you gain will be invaluable to you as a guide to the supplementary nutrients your plants require.

There are a number of available commercial fertilizers that are especially compounded for individual plant varieties such as roses,

African violets, orchids, and cacti. These special compounds are ideal for the beginner or the enthusiast who desires to restrict his floricultural activities to one specific kind of plant.

It is imperative that one establish and maintain a uniform schedule for fertilizing plants. The question frequently asked is "How much and how often?" I believe the briefest and best answer to this question is that one should always read labels, for they contain the recommendations of the manufacturer. An application of every two weeks is a direction commonly seen on many labels. It must be remembered that overfertilizing is as harmful as underfertilizing and often causes root burn.

Two important rules pertaining to the use of fertilizers are: Never use a nutrient plant food or fertilizer when a growing medium is dry; apply water first and allow time for a proper drainage period. Remember, nutrients or fertilizers should be discontinued when a plant is in its dormant period.

Pruning, Grooming, and Pinching

A houseplant, allowed to grow without inhibition, eventually reverts to its wild state. It becomes shaggy and will develop unsightly sprouts or shoots.

To be attractive, a plant should be neat and trim, and most plants are at their best when symmetrical and bushy. Pruning should not consist of random chopping or generalized slashing, but a gentle technique of snipping up and down and around the plant, ever striving to create bushiness. Between prunings, undesirable sprouts should be removed.

A special form of pruning is called pinching and is used for the removal of tips. This helps to keep a plant symmetrical, controls its height, and aids budding and flowering. Most begonias, geraniums, coleuses, and philodendrons are well-known plants that benefit from pinching.

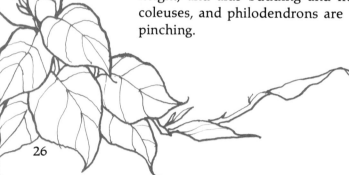

26

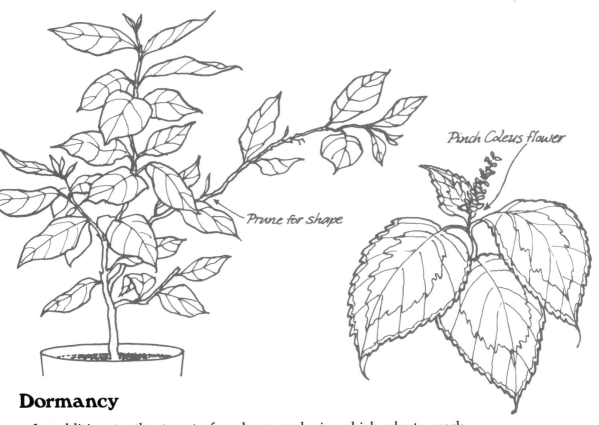

Prune for shape

Pinch Coleus flower

Dormancy

In addition to the twenty-four-hour cycle in which plants work feverishly during the hours of light, then eat and rest during the hours of darkness, most plants have periodic intervals when they rest more profoundly. At this time, their growth is practically at a standstill, and they cease to flower or set buds. These intervals are referred to as dormant periods. The duration of dormancy varies from plant to plant. Many bulb plants, for example, remain totally dormant for months, whereas the majority of geraniums do not exhibit a definite dormant period but continually grow and bud, and the African violet blooms without interruption when it is in an environment of its liking. Most plants enter a dormant period shortly after they have bloomed. During dormancy a plant generally exhibits signs of a slowing down of its metabolism such as growth stoppage, slight change of leaf coloring, and mild drooping. A dormant plant requires little or no sun, limited watering, and absolute cessation of fertilization. It should never be repotted during dormancy or have its root system disturbed in any way.

Disease

An ornamental houseplant seldom becomes diseased with proper care. The neglected plant is the vulnerable plant. If it is forced to exist in an arid environment, placed in an area devoid of light, potted in a container without proper drainage, over- or underwatered, or over- or underfertilized, a plant is in danger.

Placing a plant in a growing medium that is excessively acid or alkaline can result in disease and even death. For those who do not use commercial mixes and desire to measure the relative acidity or alkalinity of their homemade soil mixtures, there are chemical soil-testing kits available. These kits determine the intensity or degree of acidity or alkalinity, which is expressed by the chemical symbol pH and when accompanied by a numeral such as 7, is then referred to as a pH value. If one visualizes a scale with numerals from 0 to 14, 7 obviously will be exactly in the middle. The pH value scale is the same, and the numeral 7 is designated neutral. A reading of 7 is interpreted to be neither acid nor alkaline. The lower down the scale below 7, the more acid, and the higher on the scale above 7, the more alkaline. Most houseplants thrive in a medium that is neutral or slightly acid (pH6 to pH7).

A few acid-loving plants that do better in a growing medium that has a lower pH value than 7 are the amaryllis, the azalea, the begonia, the calla lily, the cyclamen, the fern, the gardenia, the geranium, the hydrangea, and the primrose.

Houseplants that require a growing medium of a higher pH value than 7, or one that is slightly alkaline, are few in number; the most common are the acacia, the cineraria, the heliotrope, the hibiscus, the ivy, the poinsettia, and the swainsona.

Disease prevention and control are essential. Sick plants are usually very difficult to cure. Worthwhile practices for the prevention and control of plant disease are as follows: Practice proper plant hygiene by using clean pots and removing dead leaves and branches regularly. Keep the physical environment sanitary and isolate or discard diseased plants without delay or remorse.

Signs and symptoms of plant diseases do not have to be enumerated, because one has only to remember that a diseased plant looks sick and acts sick. One should be constantly alert to the fact that plant diseases may be contagious and that a sick plant should not be allowed to remain with its companions.

Those who delve further into plant pathology will find that the most common houseplant diseases are mildew, fungus, mold, and rot.

Destructive Pests

Immediate action must be taken upon the discovery of the first signs of plant infestation. After identifying the destructive insect, give the infested plant a sink spraying and allow it to dry. Keep the contaminated plant isolated. Look over your insecticides, read the labels, and if the kind you have does not mention the enemy in question, visit your garden center, find one that does, and then follow its directions explicitly.

The following list of the most commonly encountered pests should furnish the reader with sufficient information to enable him to detect insect infestation early enough to protect his valued collection.

Aphids (Plant Lice)

These culprits are minute bugs of black, green, or gray color that accumulate in piles at the end of stems. Aphids are voracious suckers capable of sapping a plant's vitality.

Mealybugs

Mealybug infestation results in cotton-white clumps adhering to the joints of a plant or the underside of its leaves. Upon early detection, it is possible to pick off the clumplike colonies of these sucking insects by means of cotton applicators dipped in rubbing alcohol.

Red Spiders

These houseplant pests result in foliage spotting and have the appearance of paprika sprinkled along a plant's stem or upon its leaves. Red-spider infestation is very common, and these pests are of the sucking variety.

Scales

Scale infestation is recognized by groups of white, gray, or brownish hump-shaped masses. Scales are sucking insects.

Thrips

Due to their minute size, thrips are barely perceptible. With the aid of a magnifying glass, they appear to be brown, black, or yellowish specks. Thrips are destructive sucking pests.

White Flies

White flies are probably one of the easiest insects to detect, for upon the slightest contact with an infected plant, colonies of them will fly off the plant and hover around it in an agitated manner and in due time will return to their hiding places on the undersurface of the plant's leaves. White flies are greedy suckers.

Plant Propagation

"Choose such pleasures as recreate much and cost little."
—RICHARD FULLER (1804–1876)

Of all the horticultural procedures, none is as fascinating or intriguing as plant propagation. Nothing is quite comparable to the joy and satisfaction of seeing your very own crisp green seedlings emerging from the growing medium upon which, a few days previously, you cast several tiny life-giving pellets. What could be as gratifying as the satisfaction of seeing tiny leaflets budding from the cuttings that you only recently inserted into a growing medium with the fond anticipation of their taking root. The propagation of leaf cuttings also affords an abundance of pleasure and delight.

Back in Granny's day, discarded coffee cans, old pie or cake pans, soup dishes, and a score of other household receptacles were used to germinate plants from seed. Granny had to make her own medium for growing seeds, and if you are a modern do-it-yourself stalwart, you might attempt to mix two parts loam, one part humus or leaf mold, and one part sand. This mixture was very popular during Granny's era, and if not exactly Granny's formula, I am confident it will be an ideal substitute. In this age of urban living it is becoming progressively more difficult to obtain the necessary ingredients for growing media. We are fortunate, however, that botanical scientists have greatly reduced the labor required in former years for seed germination and have practically eliminated the complications commonly encountered in the past.

We limit our discussion of propagation to the most common methods: by seed, by cuttings, by division, and by stolons.

Propagation by Seed

Plant propagation from seed is the most exciting manner of increasing one's collection and probably the most satisfying. I trust it will be recalled that I recommend the use of commercial soil mixtures and preferably soilless mixtures as a sowing medium as opposed to modifying one's garden topsoil. In addition to various commercial soil mixtures, a number of other types of preparations for growing seedlings are obtainable. Milled sphagnum moss, an organic substance, is clean to handle and requires only the addition of water to render it ready for use. Vermiculite from mica is a very popular medium, especially the seed-sowing brand Terra-Lite, a product that possesses unusual moisture-retaining properties, and Perlite, a product made from volcanic ash, which has unusual cooling properties. Many authorities advocate a combination of equal parts of these three preparations, which takes advantage of the good qualities of each of them and provides an all-purpose sowing mixture.

Over the past decade, horticultural preparations and procedures have been scientifically perfected to the point where it is no longer necessary to take the time to prepare a sowing mixture or even, in some cases, to find a container in which to put it. Organic sowing and growing mixtures are now commercially pressed into cubes and other shapes, which serve the threefold purpose of growing medium, container, and nutrient. You merely add water to each dry cube, sow one to three seeds per cube, depending upon the size of seed being used, and then place the seeded nutrient organic cube in a container or plastic holding tray. After germination has taken place, the plantlet is ready for transplanting to a larger container or outdoors. It is simply transferred in its organic container, thus avoiding injury.

One of the most modern and ingenious horticultural improvements for seed germination is a flatly compressed organic disk held in a net. It is approximately the size of a silver dollar, and if dropped in water, the disk will swell up to approximately seven times its thickness in a very few minutes. With the permission of the George W. Park Seed Company, I include the following excerpt from their catalog, which graphically describes the product that they call Park's One-Step.

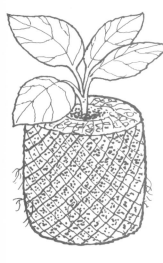

"One-Step" is a new concept in producing plants ready for the garden. Just add water to each "One-Step" and stand back. They will expand to seven times their height in minutes. Drop a few seeds on each "One-Step" and give light and moisture until plants are ready for the garden. Roots grow right through the plastic net into the soil. Ideal for starting all plants. Park's "One-Step" makes starting from seed so clean and easy, success so sure, you will have fun raising your own plants.

As previously stated, a myriad of assorted receptacles of all sizes, shapes, and compositions have been used over the years to hold sowing media during seed germination. The same is true today, for as long as a container will hold 2 to 3 inches of sowing media, it will usually serve the purpose.

With the introduction of plastics, modern horticultural technology has produced many good new products for seed germination and for growing plants. No longer is it necessary to go through the drudgery of washing and scrubbing dirty, old red-clay pots or to build and lift heavy flats, for today we have plastic and other new, light, durable, and strong products that eliminate much of the work. If you have not perused current full-color catalogs of some of the better plant producers and suppliers, by all means do so, for they are a plant lover's dream come true. Their accessory sections vividly illustrate countless innovations and many desirable improvements.

Today, miniature plastic greenhouses are earning raves. With a supply of soilless mix and one of these little greenhouses, you can obtain a percentage of seed germination equal to the professionals. Each spring, I have at least a half dozen of these amazing gadgets in action, producing hearty tomato seedlings for friends and relatives and for personal use.

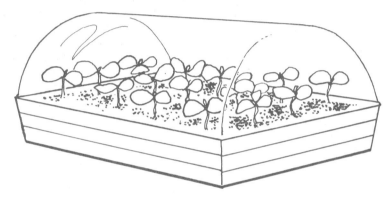

Since it is obviously impossible to deal specifically with thousands of seeds, we confine the remainder of our discussion of plant propagation by seed to the following general procedures and recommendations. If you desire to take advantage of the modern accessories such as soil mixtures, containers, and miniature plastic greenhouses, follow the manufacturer's directions explicitly. They contain not only essential directions but also a wealth of worthwhile horticultural facts. If you elect to use the techniques of two decades ago, do not forget to pasteurize or sterilize your homemade soil mixture and to scrub your clay pots with a detergent. Guard against overwatering your sowing mixture during germination; keep it moist but not flooded. Keep your germinating-seed pans, flats, or pots in a well-lighted area but not in full sun until the tiny seedlings have emerged from the surface of the medium, and transplant the seedlings as soon as they sprout their second set of leaves. Finally, protect your growing seedlings from drafts, blasts of hot air, excessive drops in temperature, and exposure to cooking-gas fumes.

If I were asked what is the most important factor in the cultivation of seedlings besides light, water, warmth, and soil, I would unhesitatingly respond, proper drainage. Provide all the essential elements and overlook proper drainage, and you will invariably end up with sick seedlings. Continue the abuse, and you will most assuredly lose them all. The prevention of such a situation is accomplished by making certain that before seed germination is attempted, the container to be used has a provision for proper drainage. First inspect the bottom of the container, pot, or receptacle and make certain that it has an aperture large enough to prevent water accumulation. In addition, put a few layers of broken pot shards, pebbles, driveway gravel, pieces of glass,

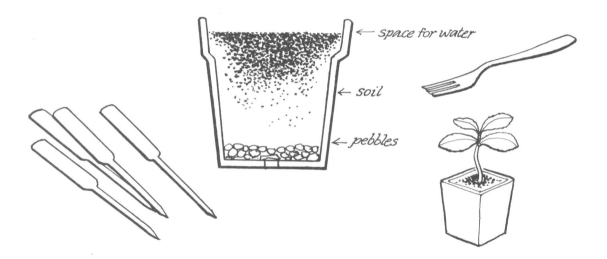

← space for water

← soil

← pebbles

or ceramic material into the bottom of the container and fill with a potting medium, leaving a space of at least one-half inch at the top for watering and applying nutrients.

The proper time for transplanting a seedling is a subject long debated. Numerous camps of thought exist, each promulgating their specific techniques. I concur with the majority and recommend waiting for a seedling to sprout or produce its second set of leaves.

When your seedlings are ready for transplanting and you have a growing medium of your choice prepared, tenderly lift the delicate seedlings out of the medium with a small fork or those plastic or wooden markers that are used to identify plants and gently transfer them.

34

Propagation by Division

Many plants may be reproduced easily by separating them into sections or portions. Plants that develop in clusters or irregular masses such as the spider plant, the African violet, and several varieties of ferns are ideal for this method of propagation. The mature plant must be divided in such a way that each portion retains some of the root system and part of the plant's crown. This can usually be accomplished by gently pulling the sections apart, but a sharp knife may be required for woody or heavily matted plants.

Propagation by Stolons

The production of runners or stolons is characteristic of certain plants. These shoots readily take root in the soil of the parent plant and on occasion manage to reach over and take hold in the pot of a neighboring plant. If allowed to remain, they will gradually develop into plantlets, and then the runners can be cut and the new plants put into containers of their own. It is also possible to reproduce from stolons by cutting about three inches off the ends of them and transplanting as you would cuttings.

Propagation by Stem or Leaf Cuttings

Without question the simplest and most common method of plant propagation is by means of cuttings, sometimes referred to as slips. The modus operandi is as follows: Cut a healthy four- to five-inch slip diagonally with a sharp knife or razor. Cut off the leaves of its lower two inches and remove all existing buds. After dipping the cutting into a hormone powder such as Rootone, insert it two to three inches deep in a moist rooting medium. The slip and its container should then be placed in a plastic bag or plastic miniature greenhouse and put in good light, but not direct sun, until new growth indicates successful rooting.

35

Little wonder that I am so enthusiastic about miniature plastic greenhouses, for in my experience I have enjoyed an unusually high percentage of successful rooting using these novel floricultural innovations.

Many hobbyists root some of their cuttings in water, a workable method for philodendron, water ivy, and certain begonias. Propagation in moist sand or a prepared rooting mix is a much more reliable method, however, for rooting the majority of stem cuttings.

Some plants are capable of being reproduced by leaf cutting, among them African violets, jade plants, gloxinias, peperomias, certain begonias, and snake plants. Leaf-cutting propagation is accomplished as follows: Take a rex begonia leaf, for example, make straight incisions with a razor blade across a few of the leaf's veins on the underside, and gently press the prepared leaf upon the surface of a moist medium. Add weight to the leaf cutting by placing a small piece of a broken pot or pebble upon its surface, and eventually plantlets will begin to develop wherever the razor-blade incisions were made.

Plants for Flowering

Leaf and flower forms are varied.

38

African Violet

(Saintpaulia)

Without doubt the African violet is the most popular of all houseplants and has held this distinction for many years. Its popularity is proved by the fact that it is difficult to find a town or city that does not have an African violet society.

A native to Africa and a member of the gesneria family, it blooms abundantly, and its countless enchanting cultivars are of the single, double, or semidouble type. They are available in delightful shades of purple, violet, blue, white, red, and pink. The plant is a low grower and usually matures into a perfect rosette. Its rich-green leaves are of various shades and shapes.

The violet thrives in an area offering a north, east, or west exposure and does poorly in full sun. Its leaves are apt to turn yellow if a plant is exposed to the intense rays of a summer sun. One can overcome possible sun damage by covering a plant with a semitransparent material, such as paper or cheesecloth, during the hours of full sun.

Tepid water should be used, but one should be careful not to spatter water on a violet's foliage. Bottom watering is better, therefore, than surface watering. The plant thrives in high humidity. Daily room ventilation is very desirable, but drafts must be avoided.

The African violet may be cultivated in garden topsoil mixed with leaf mold and sand. The average houseplant enthusiast will find, however, that the special commercial African violet mixtures are safer and more reliable. The plant enjoys being pot-bound. African violet fertilizers are available under several labels and are most effective.

The African violet is a warmth-lover and does well in a day temperature as high as 80° F. and a night temperature as low as 65° F. The violet is readily propagated by means of leaf cuttings, plant division, or seed. It is vulnerable to a number of pests.

Amaryllis

(Hippeastrum)

The various cultivars of the stately bulbaceous amaryllis produce enormous flowers in a gorgeous range of colors including white, cream, purple, pink, and red. The amaryllis blooms measure five to eight inches. The plant is native to South Africa and is truly the king of the flowering houseplants. The majority of amaryllis plants attain a height of twenty-four to thirty inches.

Amaryllis bulbs are potted singly in relatively small pots. One should allow only a small space between the bulb and the inner surface of its container. The upper end of the bulb should be above the surface of the potting soil. Garden topsoil is usually satisfactory as a growing medium, but a commercial all-purpose potting-soil mix is safer and more reliable. For the apartment dweller who desires to grow the beautiful amaryllis, the most convenient way would be to purchase a preplanted giant Dutch amaryllis, which will require only watering.

The ideal planting time for amaryllis bulbs is during October or November. After a bulb has been potted and its soil moistened, it should be removed to some area that is cooler and darker than one's living quarters. A corner of a cellar is usually ideal. While the planted bulb is in the dark, it should be kept practically dry. It usually takes a month for a bulb to grow a six- to eight-inch sprout and for it to develop an adequate root system. When this stage of growth has been attained, the baby plant is removed from its dark location, placed in full sun, and watered liberally.

The novice will be astonished to see the rapidity with which an amaryllis grows from the six-inch sprout stage into a mature plant. He will also have difficulty believing that he has been instrumental in cultivating the enormous and magnificently beautiful flowers before his eyes and above all comprehending how all of this has taken place in but a few weeks.

After flowering, one should strive to preserve the plant's foliage as long as possible to allow it to manufacture and store food for its next blooming period. Eventually, the foliage will lose its color, which is a sign that the plant is entering dormancy, which usually lasts for a period of approximately three months, and at this time the soil should be allowed to remain practically dry. During the dormant period, which occurs in the summer months, one can bury the resting plant, in its container, in a moderately shaded area of the garden, or it may be kept indoors close to a window having a north, east, or west exposure. At the end of dormancy one will discover new sprouting, which indicates it is time to replant the bulb in a new batch of growing soil and to repeat the steps necessary to produce another superb and spectacular amaryllis. The amaryllis may be propagated by seed.

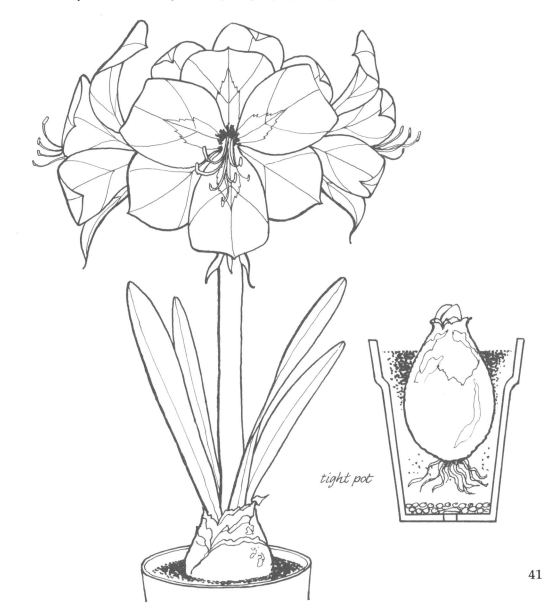

tight pot

41

Amazon Lily

(Eucharis grandiflora)

The Amazon lily, native to Central America, is a wild flowering plant that grows en masse over widespread areas. It is a bulbaceous plant that may bloom twice a year. The plant's leaves are lustrous green, and it may grow as high as two feet. The Amazon lily produces dainty fragrant white trumpet-shaped blooms usually during the winter months.

The lily requires bright light but not full sun. It flourishes in a day temperature up to 75° F., with a night temperature as low as 55° F. The plant requires more than average watering to maintain a constantly moist soil during its growing and blooming period. After blooming, the plant enters a dormant period of three to four weeks, and during this rest period water should be curtailed.

Any all-purpose commercial soil mix can be used to grow this showy plant. When potting, place a bulb in a five-inch pot with the neck of the bulb just above the surface of the soil. This can be done any month of the year. To encourage blooming, a moderate amount of nutrients should be applied once a month, and foliage should be kept moist by means of periodic misting. This plant is propagated by means of plant division.

The Amazon lily is best known for its fragrance, which has been likened to that of a tropical citrus fruit such as the lime or lemon. At the height of blooming its delightful fragrance permeates the area in which the plant is growing.

Begonia

Together with the African violet, the orchid, the geranium, and other universally popular flowers is the dainty and exquisite begonia. Although there are many outdoor garden varieties, begonia plants have been favored and coveted as houseplants throughout the world for many years.

If I were asked to name the begonia group I prefer, it would have to be the elegant *Begonia semperflorens,* commonly called the wax begonia. These plants are noted for their decorative, waxen, lustrous, deep-green or brownish-red leaves. Their blossoms are delightfully brilliant, with varieties in white and a wide range of pinks and reds. The wax begonia is a constant bloomer, and this characteristic has gained it widespread popularity. A pleasing feature of the *B. semperflorens* is its height, which seldom exceeds twelve inches.

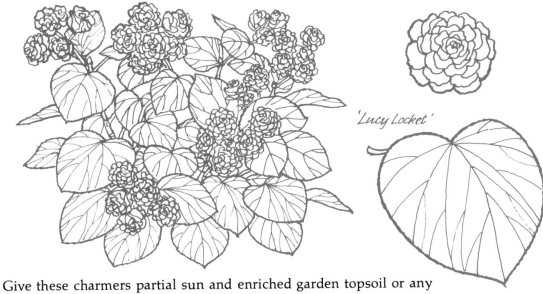

'Lucy Locket'

Give these charmers partial sun and enriched garden topsoil or any all-purpose commercial potting mix, keep their soil on the dry side, hold them pot-bound, and pinch them back to preserve bushiness. Propagation may be accomplished by cuttings or seeds. This plant will thrive in a day temperature of up to 75° F. and a night temperature as low as 55° F. The plant will perform best in a humid or moist atmosphere. These general cultural requirements may be applied to the following begonia types.

43

(B. erythrophylla feastii)

The beefsteak begonia *(B. erythrophylla feastii)* is of the rhizomatous type, characterized by moderately thick round leaves having fuzzy or hairy margins. The surface of the leaf is green, and the underside is a distinct red. The blossoms are of a pale-pink hue and develop on long stems. This begonia is often used as a hanging-basket ornamental.

(B. heracleifolia)

The star begonia *(B. heracleifolia)* is another rhizomatous type and is characterized by unusually large star-shaped bronze-green leaves and dusty-pink long-stemmed flowers.

Brazilian Edelweiss

(Rechsteineria leucotricha)

The delightful Brazilian edelweiss is a comparatively low plant native to South America. It is an attractive, decorative houseplant having smoky-green hairy leaves. It bears tube-shaped blossoms of shell-pink, and its tubular flowers are usually one inch in length.

After blooming, this plant usually enters a dormant period of three or four months, during which time the plant's foliage loses its color. During dormancy the plant should be placed in a dimly lighted area and kept in a dry condition at about 60° F.

This plant is a warmth-lover and will tolerate a day temperature up to 80° F., with a night temperature as low as 60° F. It enjoys bright light and shaded sun. It requires moderate watering with comparatively dry intervals and will do well with weekly nutrient applications during flowering. Any commercially prepared soil mix is adequate, as is fortified garden topsoil. Propagation of the Brazilian edelweiss is accomplished by cuttings or seeds.

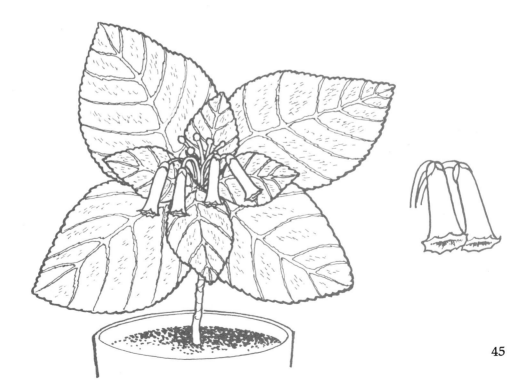

Brazilian Firecracker

(Manettia)

This vivid plant, native to South America, bears tubular-shaped flowers of bright firecracker-red with dainty yellow tips. This plant, also called the Mexican firecracker, is a climbing plant. It is most attractive when used as a hanging-basket type and develops trailers up to two feet long. The firecracker is a constant bloomer that should be kept in full sun.

The plant will adapt itself to most general soil mixtures and commercial potting mixes. It enjoys being moderately pot-bound. The plant does best in a moist soil but does not react well to "wet feet." It will do well in a day temperature as high as 75° F. and a night temperature as low as 60° F. Propagation of Brazilian firecracker plants is accomplished by cuttings.

Calla Lily

(Zantedeschia rehmannii)

The popular and dainty calla lily, of the arum family, is native to South Africa. Commonly designated as the pink dwarf, it has an average height of only eighteen inches and a charming, delicate pink shade. Nothing in flowerdom is more exquisitely textured or more impressively beautiful than regal, trumpet-shaped waxy callas. The popular pink dwarf is ideally suited for indoor cultivation.

The calla is a bulbaceous plant best grown with a single tuber in a five- or six-inch pot. The tuber is planted just deep enough so that its neck is protruding from the surface of the soil. Plants may be started indoors practically any time of year. Pot early in October for a showy bloom during the holiday season. When potted, the tuber and its container should be moved to a cool corner of a cellar or entryway and kept there for about three weeks. After this, it should be placed in an area affording full sun and soaked with tepid water. At this stage the plant will require weekly applications of any all-purpose houseplant nutrient. The calla will grow best with a day temperature as high as 70° F. and a night temperature as low as 50° F. This plant requires a rich soil, such as rich garden topsoil or any all-purpose commercial potting-soil mixture, fortified with dry manure or any all-purpose houseplant fertilizer.

After the lily has delighted you and your friends and its flowering period has come to an end, watering should be diminished over a short period of time until it is discontinued completely. At this time it has entered its deep dormant period, and the resting tuber should once again be placed in a cool dry area and allowed to regain its strength and vigor. In early fall repot the tuber using a new batch of growing medium and repeat the same steps.

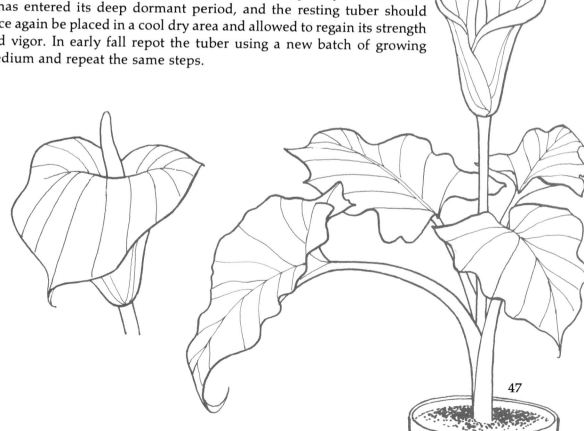

47

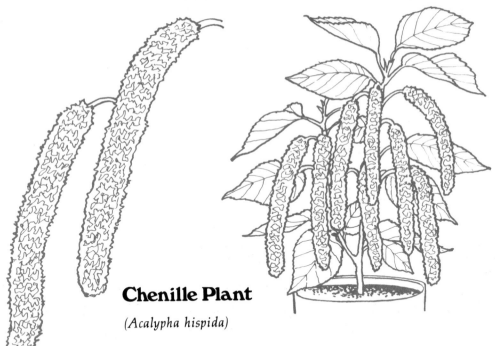

Chenille Plant

(Acalypha hispida)

The captivating chenille plant is native to the East Indies and is a member of the spurge family. It is recognized by its brilliant, cardinal-red, dangling, fuzzy blooms. This plant may attain a height of thirty inches and has a tendency to become straggly if not pruned periodically.

The attractive chenille enjoys full sun and does best with a day temperature up to 75° F. and a night temperature as low as 65° F. It demands an environment of high humidity, and its soil must be kept moist. The plant will do well when grown in any commercial all-purpose potting-soil mixture, and an application of a nutrient should be administered every two weeks during periods of active growth. This lovely plant will benefit when repotted annually, and you may propagate it by cuttings.

Fuchsia, or Lady's-Eardrop

(Fuchsia)

The fuchsia is a charming old-time favorite having many showy single or double cultivars in vivid color combinations of crimson, pink, purple, and white. Some of these plants are of the trailing type. These are colorful beauties when grown in hanging baskets. The fuchsia bears numerous attractive pendulous flowers similar to a lady's earring with

48

a dangling pendant. This plant, native to the American tropics and New Zealand, is named after Leonhard Fuchs, the renowned German botanist. It is a member of the evening-primrose family.

The fuchsia is a demanding plant. To retain its beauty and to preserve its original vitality, it requires bright light but never full sun; a cool area with a day temperature under 65° F. and a night temperature as low as 50° F.; frequent watering (from the bottom as well as from the top) to maintain a constantly moist soil; rich garden topsoil or any commercial all-purpose houseplant mixture fortified with dry manure or any all-purpose houseplant fertilizer, with supplementary nutrients every two weeks.

In late fall certain steps must be taken to preserve your fuchsia for the following year: Prune a portion of top growth; repot if necessary; place in a cool, shaded area; curtail water and allow the plant to rest until January. Propagation may be accomplished by midwinter cuttings. The common enemy of the fuchsia is the white fly.

Gardenia

(Gardenia jasminoides)

The waxy white gardenia, fragant and dainty, with thick lustrous deep-green leaves, ranks high on the list of the most beautiful flowering houseplants. Unfortunately, it is a difficult plant to manage, and its cultivation is definitely not for the novice or the weekend gardener. The popularity and beauty of the gardenia justifies its inclusion, however. It is of the madder family and native to China. Surprisingly, the gorgeous gardenia was named for an American botanist, Dr. Alexander Garden (1730–1791), of Charleston, South Carolina.

The resolute indoor gardener who takes the time and patience to nurture a gardenia plant until it matures and blooms will find the accomplishment rewarding and satisfying.

The important cultural requirements of the gardenia are full sun; a day temperature of approximately 70° F. and a night temperature as low as 60° F.; common garden topsoil with equal parts sand and peat moss, enriched with one-half part dry manure or any all-purpose soluble houseplant fertilizer; acidified potting soil; uniformly moist soil, bottom watering recommended; high humidity. The plant should be taken outdoors during the summer months; repot with fresh soil at this time; prune and groom if required; remove all buds that develop while plant remains outdoors to assure blooming during winter months; water during dry spells; and bring plant indoors before September 1. The common enemies of the gardenia are mealybugs and red spiders.

Geranium

(Pelargonium)

The geranium ranks high among popular houseplants throughout the world. Native to South Africa, the sturdy colorful pelargonium was first brought to Europe in 1632, and shortly thereafter it gained enthusiastic admiration and widespread public demand.

The numerous species and hundreds of varieties of the pelargonium range from tiny miniatures and dainty dwarfs up to the large, tree-size geraniums commonly seen in many California gardens. Some plants are desired for their brilliant colors and shades, and others for their leaf patterns and scent.

The zonal geranium *(P. hortorum)* is the common, old-fashioned garden variety that is best known and that can be encouraged to bloom during any season. Its blooms are the familiar pinks, whites, and reds seen throughout the country in gardens, planters, boxes, and countless sunny windows.

The Lady Washington, or the Martha Washington *(P. domesticum)*, is considered by many to be the largest and most beautiful of all pelargoniums. This variety commonly flowers during March or April with vivid multicolored blooms as large as four inches in diameter. the *P. domesticum* prefers a cool environment. It does best in a day temperature as high as 60° F. and a night temperature as low as 40° F.

Scented-leaved geraniums were highly valued a century ago for flavoring homemade preparations such as jellies. They were also used in bath water and often dropped into a finger bowl to give it a spicy aroma. Another common practice in those days was to dry the leaves of several varieties of scented-leaved geraniums and keep them in a jar to be sprinkled about from time to time as a room deodorant or placed in a drawer between linens or undergarments. The scented mixture was referred to as a potpourri, and no lady of those days was without a jar of her own blend of dried scented geranium leaves, which she often sewed into sachet bags to place about her home to give it an aroma of spicy freshness. Among the most popular of the scented-leaved geraniums are those having a lemon, apple, peppermint, nutmeg, cinnamon, and rose fragance.

In addition to the scented-leaved geraniums, there are fancy-leaved geraniums desired for their attractive multipatterned leaves of various shapes, sizes, and shades.

The ivy-leaved geraniums *(P. peltatum)* are little trailing gems, grown best in hanging baskets. Their glossy foliage is similar to ivy, and their many varieties offer vivid single or double flowers in pink, all shades of red, and royal purple. These plants are easily grown, and they are colorful charmers during their long blooming period between February and September.

In general, geraniums require full sunlight and should be kept moderately dry. They prefer a slightly acid growing medium and will do well in any all-purpose houseplant potting mixture or rich garden topsoil with a small amount of sand added. When in the active growing stage, geraniums should be given a nutrient once a month. The plant enjoys being pot-bound in a four- to five-inch pot, and pinching and grooming will occasionally be required to preserve bushiness and compactness. Most geraniums do best in a day temperature up to 70° F. and a night temperature as low as 50° F. Pelargoniums are comparatively pest-free. They are easily propagated by cuttings.

German Violet

(Exacum affine)

The German violet is a member of the gentian family and native to widespread tropical areas of the Old World.

The *E. affine* may grow as high as twenty-four inches and is a slow-growing, very compact, and uniformly branched plant. Its foliage is waxy green, and it produces an abundance of dainty powder-blue pleasingly fragrant flowers with throats of golden-yellow.

This showy houseplant is not overly finicky about potting soil as long as it is moderately rich. It will perform nicely in rich garden topsoil or any of the all-purpose commercial houseplant soil mixtures. I obtain excellent results with a soilless mix. The German violet requires a moist soil and enjoys a humid atmosphere.

The plant is grown from seed and flowers during the late fall, winter, and early spring months. During the blooming period applications of any all-purpose houseplant fertilizer should be administered twice a month.

The plant is a warmth-lover, requiring full sun during the fall, winter, and spring months and partial sun in the summer. It appreciates a day temperature up to 70° F., with a night temperature as low as 55° F.

I have found my exacum plants greatly appreciated and cherished as gifts by my friends, so I give them away in full bloom and grow new ones each summer.

This plant, although fairly free of pests, is not easily grown, but it is so rewarding that it is well worth the extra effort.

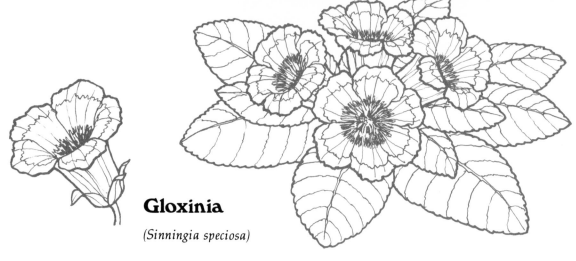

Gloxinia

(Sinningia speciosa)

This colorful, ornamental, and charming houseplant is native to Brazil. Grown from tubers, the popular species, *S. speciosa*, usually grows as high as twelve inches. Its leaves are very similar to those of the African violet, with pink or blue blooms as large as five inches in diameter.

The plant is a warmth-lover that does best in a day temperature of 70° F. and a night temperature as low as 60° F. The gloxinia requires more humidity than the average plant, does not demand full sun, and does best behind a window having an east or a west exposure.

The gloxinia, flexible as to potting soil, will thrive in any all-purpose commercial houseplant potting mix. If garden topsoil is available for potting, it should be mixed with sand and a small amount of peat moss. Use one tuber to a five-inch pot and plant just deep enough to leave the tuber's crown exposed. The ideal potting time is between January and March. Watering is best accomplished from the bottom, because one should avoid splashing water on the plant's velvety leaves. Any all-purpose houseplant fertilizer or liquid manure should be applied every two weeks during the budding and blooming periods.

One can expect blooms to develop approximately a month after potting, and blooming should continue throughout the spring. After flowering ceases, watering should be gradually curtailed, and the plant should be cut off at the soil's surface. After this, it should be stored in a dark cool area of a cellar or entryway. The tuber should be allowed to rest for approximately six to eight weeks, and its soil should be moistened sparingly and infrequently. After the end of the resting period, the tuber should be repotted. Use a pot one or two sizes larger and fresh soil. The plant should then be placed back in its original growing location and handled as before. A new flowering period will begin during October or early November. This plant may be propagated by cuttings.

Hibiscus

(Hibiscus rosa-sinensis)

Commonly called the rose of China, the hibiscus is native to China and a member of the mallow family. It is classified as a tree, but many regard it as a shrub or bush. When grown as a houseplant, it can attain a height of two to four feet. The plant is a slow grower, and its large flowers resemble hollyhocks. Its cultivars are obtainable in white, yellow, or red shades. The popular and beautiful hibiscus is the state flower of Hawaii.

This plant enjoys a location affording full sun with a day temperature up to 75° F. and a night temperature as low as 55° F. The hibiscus does not require a special potting soil and will do well in any commercial all-purpose potting soil or rich garden topsoil. The plant demands more water than the average, enjoys periodic soakings, and requires a moist soil during its blooming period. Above all, it must be kept in an environment of high humidity. Applications of a nutrient every two weeks are indicated. The hibiscus should be pruned after blooming to prevent it from becoming straggly. During the summer months this plant should be placed in a shady area either in the garden or in a corner of a breezeway. Propagation is achieved by cuttings. The red spider is this plant's main enemy.

Hydrangea

(Hydrangea macrophylla)

The beautiful hydrangea is one of the most popular Easter plants. During this spring holiday period it is featured in garden centers and supermarkets along with calla lilies, tulips, hyacinths, and other brightly colored plants. The hydrangea is of the saxifrage family and native to Japan.

The handsome cultivars of the *H. macrophylla* are recognized by their characteristic serrated waxy leaves and their compact spherical blooms, which develop into charming clusters of pink, blue, red, or white.

This handsome plant does best in a room with a day temperature as high as 70° F. and a night temperature as low as 50° F. It requires a humid environment and enjoys daily misting. This plant requires more water than the average, and its soil must be kept moist. It is often necessary to water a hydrangea more than once a day. Any all-purpose commercial houseplant growing mixture may be used, but an acidifying agent may have to be added in dealing with blue or pink varieties. An application of any all-purpose houseplant fertilizer should be given every two weeks. The plant may be placed outdoors during the summer but must be watered during dry spells. After the first frost it should be brought indoors and kept in a cool area of a cellar or entryway where there is limited light. During this dormant period the plant should be kept moderately dry by watering sparingly every three weeks. About the first of the year the dormant plant should be brought back to its original area, given bright light, and watered more frequently. When the plant exhibits renewed growth, it should be placed in full sun.

The hydrangea is not for the weekend indoor gardener, for its requirements and demands make it a difficult plant to grow.

Impatiens

(Impatiens sultanii)

This charming plant is one that Granny probably had in her collection. It was often called patience plant in those days. The plant is of the balsam family and is native to eastern Africa.

The *I. sultanii* can grow to a height of twenty inches, and when established, it rewards its proud owner with continuous blooms. This species develops waxy flowers of scarlet-red and pink shades.

This plant is commonly grown outdoors in shady summer flower beds from seed or nursery plants. It is equally ideal and desirable as a houseplant. It requires full sun in the winter. Place it behind a window affording a southern exposure. The plant does best in a day temperature up to 65° F., with a night temperature as low as 55° F. Impatiens requires a rich growing medium such as fortified garden topsoil or any of the commercial all-purpose houseplant soil mixtures. The plant requires a moist soil and does best when grown in a small-sized pot.

This showy, colorful, and almost continuous bloomer is easily grown, comparatively free of pests, and capable of being propagated from cuttings or from seeds.

Jasmine

(Jasminum grandiflorum)

The jasmine is of the olive family and might well be called the perfume plant because of its pleasant and permeating fragrance. The plant produces pink-tinged white flowers formed in dainty clusters. Somewhat difficult to manage, the jasmine requires full sun but does best in a day temperature under 65° F. and a night temperature as low as 55° F.

This plant does not need a special potting soil. Any rich garden topsoil mixed with a small amount of sand and bone meal will be sufficient, as well as any commercial all-purpose houseplant soil mixture. The soil must be kept moist, however, and the environment should be moderately humid. This can be accomplished to a certain degree by daily misting. The plant should receive an application of liquid manure or any all-purpose houseplant fertilizer every two weeks.

Indoor gardeners place their jasmine plants outdoors during the summer months in an area of partial sun and return them to the house before the first frost. The plant should then be placed in a cool, dimly lit corner. Watering should be reduced, and the plant may be pruned if necessary. About the first of the year it should be watered thoroughly and given full sun. Jasmine plants may be propagated by stem cuttings. Their common enemies are mealybugs and scales.

Jessamine

(Cestrum parqui)

This species is commonly called willow-leaved jessamine, and of all the jessamine plants, this one is ideal for indoor culture and is prized for its exciting, sweet, permeating fragrance, which envelops the entire area where the plant is grown. It is a member of the nightshade family.

The plant may attain a height of three feet but will be at its best when kept to twenty inches. The *C. parqui* produces vivid green heavy-grained attractive leaves, with delicate blooms of a pale greenish-white hue. The plant usually blooms in early January.

It will do well in a window affording partial sun, but during colder months the plant should be placed in full sun. It is a warmth-lover and enjoys a day temperature as high as 75° F. and a night temperature as low as 55°F. The jessamine is not finicky as to potting soil, and it will do well in rich garden topsoil or in any of the all-purpose commercial soil mixtures. The plant requires a moderately humid atmosphere that may be attained by daily foliage spraying, and its soil should be kept uniformly moist. This jessamine species can be propagated early in the spring by cuttings.

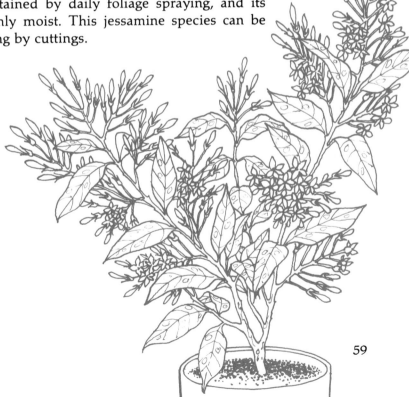

59

Kaffir Lily

(Clivia miniata)

In midspring this regal lady is a dazzling beauty when fully adorned with her large fragrant flowers of burnt orange. She may attain a height of eighteen to twenty-four inches and will dominate the area in which she is growing with her spicelike fragance. The Kaffir lily will develop and perform best when grown in partial sunlight such as behind a window with an eastern exposure. A day temperature of 70° F., with a night temperature as low as 55° F., is ideal. The plant requires rich topsoil fortified with manure or any all-purpose houseplant fertilizer. Any all-purpose houseplant soil mixture will also be sufficient if properly fortified. The plant should be watered heavily during its growing period and lightly at other times.

After the plant ceases to bloom and its beautiful flowers wither, it should be placed in an area of subdued light. When the danger of frost has passed, it can be placed outdoors in a moderately shaded area and kept there until early fall. At this time the plant should be placed indoors in a cold area, preferably with a temperature as low as 55° F. The plant will require only infrequent and sparse watering during this dormant period. After the first of the year it should be returned to its original place.

This plant enjoys being moderately pot-bound; a five- to eight-inch pot is usually adequate. Propagation of this eye-catching beauty is accomplished by division.

Lemon Tree

(Citrus limonia ponderosa)

The lemon tree is a member of the citrus family, which includes lime and orange trees as well. The *C. limonia ponderosa* produces heavily scented white flowers, shiny deep-green foliage, and yellow fruit. The fruit of this species is usually larger and heavier than most others. The ponderosa is best grown in a wooden tub, and it may attain a height of four feet.

The plant does best in a day temperature as high as 60° F. and a night temperature as low as 55° F. This is a cool plant, and to fulfill its temperature requirements, it is best grown in a sun-room or jalousied porch with a southern exposure. This plant or tree demands an acid soil, and to maintain such a pH level, one should use an acidifying agent such as diluted vinegar, which is acetic acid, or any of the commercial soluble acidifying preparations such as Stern's Miracid, which is also a 30–10–10 plant nutrient. The potting medium used may be a mixture of rich garden topsoil fortified with liquid manure or any houseplant fertilizer or any all-purpose houseplant soil mixture, which should be fortified in the same manner. The lemon tree does best when its soil is kept moist during blooming and fruit-growing periods and moderately dry at other times.

This plant, whose common enemy is the red spider, may be propagated by cuttings and also can be grown from seed.

The cultural requirements for the lime and orange trees are essentially the same as for the *C. limonia ponderosa.*

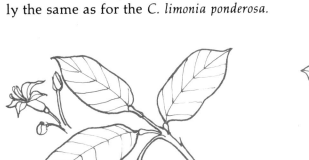

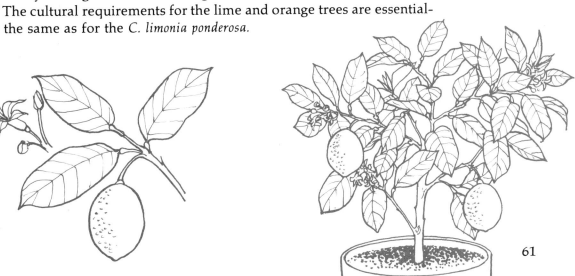

61

Living-Vase Plant

(Aechmea fasciata)

This plant is of the pineapple family and is native to South America. It is called living-vase plant because the formation of its vividly colored curved leaves gives the appearance of an ornamental vase. The *A. fasciata* is a vigorous, virtually care-free show-off that blooms from late spring on into the summer. It bears dusty-pink bracts that offer a contrast to its pale-blue flowers. The plant will usually attain a height of twenty-four inches.

As long as it receives an abundance of light, this plant will perform with little sun. A window with an east or even a west exposure will be sufficient to meet these light requirements. The temperature range found in the average home or apartment is generally acceptable providing the day temperature does not exceed 75° F. and the night temperature remains above 60° F. The plant does best with a uniformly moist soil and a moderately humid environment. Frequent foliage spraying or misting will help to maintain the desired humidity. It is also beneficial to the plant if water is allowed to remain within its leaves. The potting soil in which to grow the living-vase plant should be richer than average. Rich garden topsoil modified with peat moss and sand and well fortified with manure will usually produce good results. Any commercial all-purpose potting-soil mix is excellent providing it is enriched with manure.

This plant has a tendency to develop offshoots, or suckers, and propagation can be accomplished by removing and rooting these offshoots.

Mistletoe Fig

(Ficus diversifolia)

This ornamental houseplant is native to Malaya and a member of the mulberry family. It may attain a height of three feet but is at its best when kept at approximately twenty inches by pruning. The mistletoe fig deserves a place among the flowering plants, for it is a prolific producer of long-lasting, attractive, small, pear-shaped fruit, making it a most desirable houseplant.

This plant is best grown in bright light but not necessarily full sun. Nondemanding as to soil, it will do well in garden topsoil or any commercial all-purpose potting soil. Any all-purpose houseplant nutrient once a month will be adequate. It is a warm plant and will withstand a day temperature up to 75° F. and a night temperature as low as 60° F. The plant requires a uniformly moist soil but should be given an occasional short drying-out period. The mistletoe fig is an ideal houseplant for the working person, because its rugged nature makes it virtually care-free. It may be propagated by leaf cuttings with ease.

Oleander

(Nerium oleander)

This plant is native to Asia Minor and a member of the dogbane family. It flowers plentifully when properly cultivated, and its vivid cultivars are obtainable in pink, apricot, or white shades. The blooming period of this flower usually takes place during the spring and extends into the summer. The plant can attain a height of five feet, making it an ideal plant for a sun-room or glass-enclosed porch providing there are facilities for artificial heating.

The oleander is a sun-lover, requiring full sun. It does best in a day temperature as high as 75° F. and a night temperature as low as 55° F. Either rich garden topsoil or any all-purpose commercial potting mix will be sufficient if fortified with dry manure or any all-purpose houseplant nutrient. This plant demands more water than the average, and its soil should be moist to the touch during its blooming period. Thereafter, watering should be curtailed. Pruning should be done late in the fall. Keep the plant in a moderately cool area during its winter dormant period and water it only once a month. Tub culture is ideal for this plant, and propagation is usually accomplished by cuttings.

Passionflower

(Passiflora caerulea)

The passionflower is not a houseplant per se but an ornamental vine often referred to as the passion vine. Because this vine will grow five to six feet long, it is not a desirable window ornamental. When tub-grown, however, it can be a real charmer, especially if placed on a glass-enclosed porch and allowed to grow without inhibition as a trailing vine.

The passion is not easily grown but is presented in this book because of the interesting ancient legends connected with it. The most often repeated fable concerns certain aspects of the crucifixion of Christ and more specifically the fancied contention that the flower's structural parts resemble not only the crown of thorns but also the nails of the cross and the ten faithful apostles. For those with an available growing area plus the fortitude to tackle the management of this flowering vine, we present the following list of cultural demands: full sun; enriched, fortified garden topsoil or any of the all-purpose commercial houseplant soil mixes; uniformly moist soil; moderately high humidity; day temperature not over 75° F., with a night temperature as low as 50° F.; pruning after blooming; ninety days' rest in a cool area until new sprouting is observed, at which time it can be returned to its original growing area.

The vine is of the passionflower family and native to Brazil. It can be grown from seed or propagated by spring cuttings.

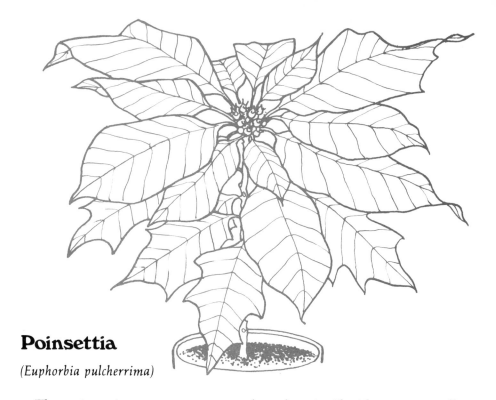

Poinsettia

(Euphorbia pulcherrima)

The poinsettia, common as a garden plant in Florida, was actually imported from Mexico around 1830. It is a member of the spurge family. Many beautiful cultivars have been developed such as the Mikkelsen varieties. The most popular of these is the brilliant-red plant so much in evidence at Christmas. Even though the poinsettia is a difficult houseplant to manage, it is so often given and received during the holidays that it deserves more than a brief discussion. Indoor gardeners, especially, will want to keep their beautiful plants alive and well for another season.

The poinsettia is not valued for its flowers but for its brilliantly colored leaves, or bracts. These can be white, pink, variegated pink, and cream as well as the familiar intense red. Enclosed in the center of these dramatically colored bracts are the inconspicuous, tiny flowers.

Less flexible than most houseplants, the poinsettia demands certain cultural conditions such as full sun and, ideally, a day temperature up to 65° F. and a night temperature as low as 55° F.; enriched garden topsoil or fortified all-purpose commercial potting soil; careful watering so that the soil is kept moderately dry but frequent misting to maintain an atmosphere of high humidity; daily ventilation but protection from injurious drafts.

When the plant completes its blooming stage, it begins to cast off its leaves. This is the start of the dormant period. Now the poinsettia requires curtailment of water until potting soil is practically dry and once-a-month watering thereafter; placement in a cool, shaded area such as a cellar or entryway.

In early spring the poinsettia can be pruned back to four to six inches and repotted. At this time it must be watered thoroughly and placed in a sunny window. When the danger of frost is past, the plant may be taken outside and placed, with its pot below the ground, in a sunny area. During dry periods it should be watered frequently. It should be returned indoors before the first frost.

Even after all this attention, the complex poinsettia needs more coddling. About the middle of October it must be put on a program of short days and long nights. This may be accomplished by allowing the plant only ten hours of daylight and placing it in complete darkness for the remaining fourteen hours. This is necessary to stimulate budding. Failing to observe these "short day" requirements, during this critical period, can mean the difference between success and failure. For the inveterate poinsettia enthusiast, propagation may be accomplished by cuttings.

Primrose

(Primula)

This colorful houseplant should be considered an annual, for the plant is such a vigorous and constant bloomer that its vitality and strength are depleted in a single season, and it never regains its original robust growing ability. The plant is an old-time favorite, gaily colorful, and when properly grown a real conversation piece.

Unfortunately, the primrose has fallen into disfavor because one of its species, *P. obconica,* is capable of causing contact dermatitis if one is allergic to it. Long before allergic manifestations were understood, the folks of yore began to call all primrose family members poison primrose plants, and the beautiful but unfairly maligned primrose suffered widespread loss of favor and popularity.

There are two common species of this houseplant that are often selected as gifts. One is the *P. malacoides,* with cultivars that bear flower clusters in a wide range of colors such as white, rose, purplish-blue, and red shades. This primrose plant is commonly called fairy primrose or baby primrose and may attain a height of twelve to twenty-four inches. The second popular primrose species is the *P. sinensis,* or the Chinese primrose, which may also attain a height up to twenty-four inches, with cultivars that bear many vividly colored flowering clusters.

The primrose does best in a cooler environment than the average houseplant and enjoys a day temperature as low as 55° F., with a night temperature as low as 45° F. When grown in a greenhouse, this showy plant is usually placed in the cooler areas. These are the ideal conditions for cultivating primrose plants, and in no way is it implied that a primrose will not perform under other conditions, for the plant will tolerate temperatures up to 65° F. providing that its other requirements are fulfilled. These are as follows: the brightest light possible without full sun, such as may be obtained behind windows with either an east or a west exposure; placement on a jalousied or glass-enclosed porch; more water than the average houseplant (soil should always be moist to touch, and bottom watering is preferable); indirect ventilation daily; any rich potting soil that has been fortified with dry manure.

Again, this plant should be considered an annual and discarded after its long blooming period. New plants are easily grown from seed, which makes it possible to have vigorously growing plantlets at all times.

Rose Miniature

(Rosa chinensis minima)

Delightful little replicas of their big sisters, the rose miniature plants are real charmers. They produce tiny buds that develop miniature roses measuring approximately three quarters of an inch in diameter. Varieties are obtainable in numerous colors such as pure white, golden-yellow, ruby-red, light pink, dark pink, double red, burgundy, and white-centered red.

It is best to order your miniature rose bushes from your favorite nursery or houseplant dealer late in the winter so that they may be placed in full sun as soon as delivered. Shortly thereafter, exquisite, dainty miniature roses will reward you with a colorful display that will continue throughout the spring. The miniature rose bushes usually grow from three to six inches, although there are varieties that may grow as high as fifteen inches.

A rose bush should be treated as a cool plant and kept in a day temperature of 65° F. and a night temperature as low as 55° F. The plant enjoys daily ventilation. Roses require rich garden topsoil or any all-purpose houseplant mix fortified with dry manure or any houseplant nutrient. The bush does not like to be pot-bound and will do best in a five- to six-inch pot. Its soil must be kept uniformly moist. The plant will do best when watered from the bottom and kept in a humid environment. Your roses may be placed in a sunny area of your garden for the summer but must be kept watered during dry periods. Early in the fall, before the first frost, the bushes should be taken indoors, pruned for uniformity, and placed in partial sun in a cool area such as an enclosed porch. At this time of rest the plant should be watered infrequently and sparsely. Around the first of the year your miniatures should be returned to their usual growing area with full sun and treated as before.

The common enemy of the miniature rose bush is the red spider. The bush may be propagated by cuttings.

The miniature rose is an exacting plant, but if one has the time to grow it properly, the end results will be rewarding and joyful.

Sensitive Plant

(Mimosa pudica)

This strange, sensitive plant is of the family Leguminosae and native to Central America. The *M. pudica* folds its leaves and droops its stalks immediately following the slightest contact, taking on a completely withered or wilted appearance. This curious reaction appears to be a possumlike, protective ruse of feigning death, because shortly thereafter the plant recuperates completely and becomes as perky and robust as it was before. The plant produces clusters of small, compact lavender flowers that form in tiny globes.

A sensitive plant enjoys full sun and needs potting soil fortified with manure or any all-purpose commercial fertilizer. It is a warmth-lover that enjoys a day temperature as high as 75° F. and a night temperature as low as 60° F. The plant's soil should be kept uniformly moist, and daily spraying or misting is recommended.

The mature and properly cultivated sensitive plant will usually grow to a height of twelve to fourteen inches. I recommend propagation of this plant by seed, and it should be treated as an annual.

Shrimp Plant

(Beloperone guttata)

The fascinating shrimp plant, a member of the Acanthus family, is native to Mexico and South America. This flexible, essentially care-free charmer is a joy for the weekend gardener who has neither the time nor the inclination to attempt the cultivation of some of the more demanding plants.

The average shrimp plant is comparatively tall and may attain a height of two to three feet. The most popular shrimp plant species is the *B. guttata,* which produces thin coral-pink or shrimp-colored overlapping bracts. These are delicately transparent, and from them many tiny white flowers appear. These blooms continue from early winter until midspring.

The shrimp plant is a warmth-lover that should be given full sun and will perform best in a day temperature up to 75° F. and a night temperature as low as 55° F. The *B. guttata* requires a rich soil mixture such as fortified garden topsoil or any of the commercial all-purpose houseplant growing mixtures to which liquid manure or any all-purpose houseplant fertilizer has been added. The plant's soil should be kept uniformly moist, and frequent sink-soaking sessions are ideal providing that they are followed by short drying-out periods in the interim. The plant will do best with monthly applications of any all-purpose soluble houseplant fertilizer.

After the plant's blooming period, it should have vigorous pruning to prevent straggling. Some gardeners summer their shrimp plant outdoors, returning it to their indoor growing area before the first frost. Propagation of this plant is accomplished by cuttings.

71

Sweet Olive

(Osmanthus fragrans)

The sweet olive is of the olive family and native to Southeast Asia. This evergreen shrub produces pleasantly fragrant white flowers that bud and bloom several times throughout the year.

The plant does well in either full or partial sun, with a day temperature as high as 70° F. and a night temperature as low as 60° F. It requires a rich potting soil such as garden topsoil or any of the commercial all-purpose houseplant potting mixtures fortified with the addition of a fertilizer. The potting soil must be kept uniformly moist, and the plant's foliage should be sprayed at least once a day to provide the necessary humid atmosphere. Flowering is actually enhanced when this plant is allowed to become pot-bound. Some gardeners take their sweet-olive plant outdoors during the summer months and place it in a partially shaded area. If this is done, care must be exercised to make sure the plant is watered during dry spells.

The sweet olive enjoys ventilation but will not tolerate a direct chilly draft. The popular *O. fragrans* grows to approximately twenty-four inches. It is not usually inclined to become straggly but may be pruned if desired. This plant is comparatively easy to manage and delightfully free of enemy pests. It may be propagated by cuttings.

Plants
for Foliage

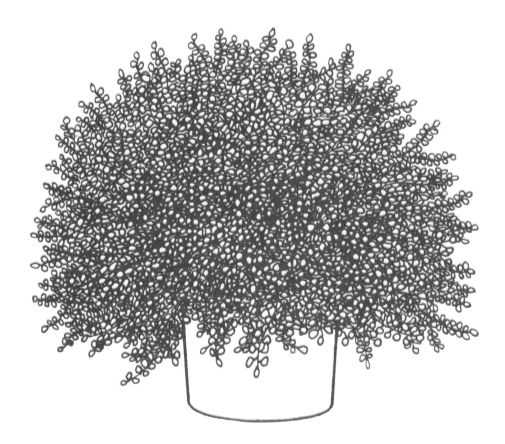

Baby's Tears

(Helxine soleirolii)

This small attractive foliage plant with numerous vivid emerald-green leaves is native to Corsica and a member of the nettle family. It is erroneously referred to as Irish moss, probably because of its widespread growth throughout Ireland.

The baby's tears is an easy plant to grow. The novice, however, should be warned of its appearance during dormancy. At this time its green foliage becomes dry, turns brown, and drops off. One should not become dismayed at the bald, unattractive stalks that remain, for within a short time, they will become laden once again with fresh tiny green leaves.

Place this little beauty in an area offering a bright light but not full sun. Rooms with an east or a west exposure and a day temperature high of 72° F. and a night temperature as low as 60° F. are ideal. It enjoys an environment with a moderately high humidity. Except during the dormant period, soil must be kept uniformly moist, and weekly sink soaks are beneficial.

Any all-purpose commercial potting mix is adequate, as is rich common garden topsoil. The plant will do well with monthly applications of any all-purpose soluble nutrient according to directions. Propagation of the baby's tears is easily accomplished during its dormant period by removing small portions of the dry stalks and inserting them in moist soil. It is virtually enemy-free.

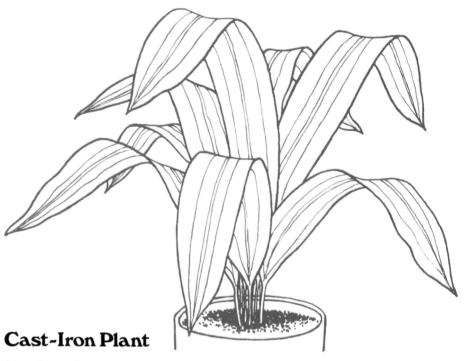

Cast-Iron Plant

(Aspidistra elatior)

This old-timer has been a common favorite over the years and still retains widespread popularity. It is a native to South China and a member of the lily family.

The *A. elatior* is truly a care-free plant because of its tolerance of neglect. This explains its designation, cast-iron plant. It will adjust to environmental variations that would normally injure most plants. This plant is known for its twenty-inch glossy blackish-green sharp-pointed leaves.

The plant is most flexible as to shade or sun and will even flourish when placed in an obscure corner with only the low-level light of a northern exposure. It will do well in a day temperature as high as 70° F., and a night temperature as low as 50° F. will not faze this Trojan. Its soil, which should be kept uniformly moist, may be a mixture of common garden topsoil with equal parts of sand and peat moss or any all-purpose commercial potting-soil mix. The aspidistra will reward its owner with handsome growth if given liquid manure or an application of any of the all-purpose potted plant fertilizers once a month. The plant is virtually enemy-free and may be propagated by means of crown division.

Chinese Evergreen

(Aglaonema commutatum)

The Chinese evergreen should be named "answer to a beginner's prayer," for it is one of the most flexible of all houseplants. It requires no sun and will flourish under the most adverse environmental conditions. Place a Chinese evergreen plant in a location of your choice, forget most of the do's and don'ts, render the meagerest amount of care, and sit back and enjoy the plaudits of your guests.

There are numerous species of this plant, which differ in height, color, and leaf pattern, and all offer the same flexibility and care-free cultivation. The *A. commutatum* is of intermediate height (usually two feet) and produces large glossy green leaves with platinum streaks. The plant is native to the Asian tropics and the Philippine Islands and is a member of the arum family.

This plant, which grows well in sunlight, surprisingly will grow in the most obscure corners with only indirect light or the light from a low-wattage incandescent lamp. In addition it will flourish in the warmest room in one's home and equally well in a cool corner. Neither low nor high humidity will faze this unusual plant. It will grow properly with weekly sink soaks and foliage spraying. The most popular growing medium is common garden topsoil, but the plant will do equally well in any all-purpose commercial potted-plant mix. This plant will also grow in water. The Chinese evergreen has the capacity to exist for months without supplementary nutrients but will exhibit more vigor with monthly applications of any all-purpose houseplant fertilizer. This durable foliage plant is virtually enemy-free. It is easily propagated by means of root division or by stem cuttings.

Coleus

(Coleus blumei)

The coleus, or painted-leaf plant, is an attractive and popular old-timer, and no houseplant collection is complete without it. Widely favored for its brilliant, multicolored foliage, coleus is an easily grown member of the mint family and native to Africa. The *C. blumei* offers numerous delightful cultivars with foliage in countless brilliant, variegated color combinations and of many shapes and sizes. The plant produces small blue flowers that should be removed before they produce seedlings. It is wise to pinch off shoots to maintain bushiness and a pleasing shape.

Here is a plant that thrives with its brilliant color scintillating when it is placed in an area offering full sun. It enjoys a day temperature as high as 70° F. and a night temperature as low as 55° F. The coleus will grow well in common garden topsoil or any all-purpose commercial houseplant soil mix. Regardless of the nature of the soil, it must be kept moist. An application of a houseplant nutrient twice a month will keep the coleus fresh and radiant. This plant is usually enemy-resistant except for mealybugs. It is easily propagated from seed or from cuttings of the varieties of one's choice.

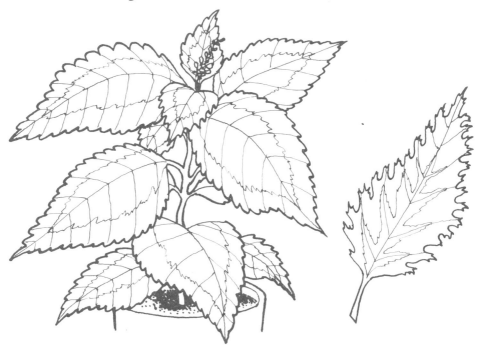

Corn Plant

(Dracaena fragrans massangeana)

This African native of the lily family obtains its common name, corn plant, from the similarity of its stalk and long, spearlike green-and-yellow-streaked foliage to that of our native corn. If left unpruned, this plant may attain tree size. The corn plant is most flexible and exceedingly rugged. Add this charmer to your collection. Pruned and trained to your liking, it is bound to evoke praise and interest.

The corn plant will grow in partially shaded areas provided there is sufficient light. It enjoys a day temperature as high as 75° F. and a night temperature as low as 55° F. Its soil should be kept moist. This plant needs an environment of high humidity, which may be provided by watering it from the bottom and placing its pot in a tray of pebbles and water. The plant calls for no more than rich garden topsoil for a growing medium and will do well in any all-purpose commercial potting-soil mix. A monthly application of any all-purpose houseplant fertilizer will be sufficient. The corn plant is essentially enemy-free. One might, however, guard against leaf spotting by keeping its leaves as dry as possible. Propagation of this attractive ornamental may be accomplished by stem cuttings.

79

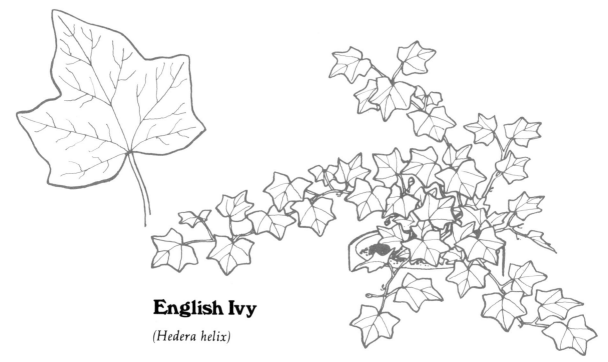

English Ivy

(Hedera helix)

English ivy is of the family Araliaceae. Probably second only to the philodendron in popularity, it is one of the most commonly seen of all trailing- or climbing-vine-type houseplants. It is at its best in a window box or hanging container. There are many varieties of English ivy, all requiring pretty much the same culture but differing in shape, size, color, and leaf markings. A healthy, well-trained, mature English ivy is a joy to behold and ideal for the beginner.

It grows poorly in full sun, preferring shaded or indirect sunlight. Failure with English ivy is most often due to keeping it in an environment that is too warm. It is a cool plant that will do best in a day temperature of 60° F. but will tolerate 70° F. Ideally, it should be placed in an area having a night temperature of 50° F. The ivy demands a moist soil and more than average humidity, which can be maintained by sink soaking and foliage misting once a week. Avoid placing English ivy in overly dry areas. This charmer will do well when planted in common garden topsoil or in any all-purpose commercial potting mix. It does not demand frequent supplemental nutrients, so a monthly application of any all-purpose houseplant fertilizer should keep this vine robust and healthy. The common enemies of the English ivy are the red spider and the aphid. New plants may be easily grown by means of cuttings.

Ferns

There are an enormous number of plants classified as Filicineae, represented by approximately 150 genera and 6,000 species that are geographically spread around the world, even in the Arctic. The majority prefer a shady growing area and do best in a humid environment, explaining why they grow so profusely in tropical forests. Few, if any, modern plants have a more ancient ancestry, for the fern's history extends back to the Paleozoic age, a fact proved by unearthed fossils.

It is such a common ornamental that detailed description would be superfluous. However, the following fern facts might be of interest. It is a plant that produces no flowers or seeds, its foliage is referred to as fronds, and reproduction is usually accomplished by asexual spores that grow in sacs on the underside or edges of the fronds. The novice often confuses spores with scale infestation, a mistake that can be avoided if one considers the innumerable spore sacs and their uniform appearance and pattern.

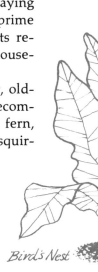

Rabbit's Foot

Ferns require good light but not full sun. They enjoy a day temperature up to 70° F., with a night temperature as low as 55° F. They will do well in any one of the commercial all-purpose houseplant soil mixes. If garden topsoil is used, it should be modified by mixing equal parts of it with sharp sand and peat moss to insure a fine, porous medium. The soil should be kept moist to touch, and a small amount of charcoal added to it periodically will help keep it sweet. Spraying or misting will help to maintain a humid atmosphere, which is a prime requisite for maintaining flourishing, healthy ferns. These plants require only infrequent nutrient applications, and any all-purpose houseplant fertilizer or diluted liquid manure will be sufficient.

There are numerous ornamental ferns. The following popular, old-time favorites have many pleasing attributes and are worthy of recommendation: asparagus fern, bird's-nest fern, Boston fern, holly fern, lace fern, maidenhair fern, Mexican tree fern, rabbit's-foot fern, squirrel's-foot fern.

Bird's Nest

Boston

81

Fiddle-Leaf Fig

(Ficus lyrata pandurata)

Luxurious, large, green, fiddle-shaped, frilly, and veined leafage is characteristic of this attractive houseplant. It is a tropical native and a member of the mulberry family. It will take reasonable periods of neglect like a stalwart. The mature fiddle fig often reaches a height of over five feet and likes to be pot-bound. A ten-inch pot is usually sufficient to maintain an established plant.

The fig will do best in areas without direct sunlight and even in remote spots providing there is sufficient bright light. It is a warmth-lover and will tolerate a day temperature as high as 75° F. and a night temperature as low as 60° F., but it should not be placed in drafts, which can cause leaf dropping. This plant does best when its soil is kept moist, and its glossy leaves will retain their healthy sheen if dust accumulation is removed occasionally by sponging. Garden topsoil is the growing medium most frequently used, but the plant does equally well in any all-purpose commercial houseplant soil mix. Liquid manure or any of the popular houseplant soluble fertilizers once a month will keep a fiddle-leaf fig robust and healthy. This plant is virtually enemy-free. It may be propagated by means of leaf cuttings.

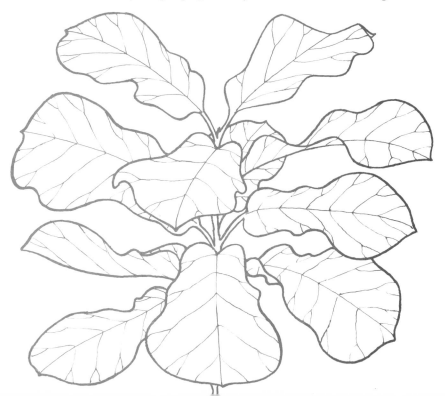

Foliage from Fruit for Fun

Here is fun for the whole family. Don't discard that large ugly avocado seed or the top of that pineapple. Save some lemon, grapefruit, or orange seeds, for with little effort on your part, they will all produce attractive foliage plants that you will be justly proud of displaying.

Avocado Plant

Take an avocado seed and root it in water or plant it in garden topsoil or any of the commercial all-purpose houseplant soil mixtures.

If you decide to root it in water, all you will need is a wide-mouth jar and four toothpicks. Partially insert the toothpicks around the upper portion of the smaller end of the seed, spikelike fashion, so they rest on the rim of the jar and support the seed. Fill the jar half full of water and place the seed broad base down into the jar. Add or remove water so that the base of the suspended seed barely touches the water's surface.

Set the rooting jar in bright light, periodically change water, and very soon you will notice roots protruding from the base of the seed. Shortly thereafter, the upper end of the seed will sprout. At this point prepare a four- to six-inch pot with garden topsoil or any commercial all-purpose houseplant soil mix, remove the toothpicks, and plant the rooted seed broad end down with the upper end just under the surface of the soil. Place the plant in a window with a bright southern exposure and keep the soil constantly moist. You will be amazed at how quickly your avocado seed will develop into an attractive four- to six-foot tropical treelike plant, with ten-inch rich-green glossy leaves. Once your avocado reaches this stage of maturity, treat it like any other flexible houseplant by providing a moderate temperature, constantly moist soil, a brightly lighted location, and monthly applications of any of the all-purpose houseplant fertilizers.

If you prefer planting the avocado seed without prerooting, be sure to plant the seed in soil with the smaller end pointing upward, just below the surface of the soil.

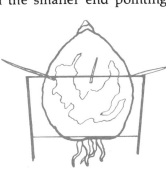

Lemon, Grapefruit, or Orange Seed Plants

Drop a few seeds in a saucer of water and allow them to stay for three to four days. Then plant them one-half inch deep in a shallow pan of premoistened soil and sand mix. Keep at 70° F. to 72° F. and in a very short period expect the emergence of attractive deep-green foliage. Keep in a location offering bright, full sun.

Pineapple Plant

Cut off the top of a pineapple with its spiky foliage, including a small portion of the fruit below. Plant this cutting approximately two inches deep in a four- to six-inch pot, using moist soil of sandy consistency. Place the pot in a warm, sunny location. If you haven't seen a potted pineapple plant, we believe you have a pleasant surprise awaiting you.

Foliage from Vegetables for Fun

Carrots, Turnips, and Beets

Foliage plants can be grown from these common kitchen vegetables. Merely cut a one-inch piece off the top end of each vegetable. Prepare a shallow bowl of pebbles, gravel, or small stones and place the vegetable ends on top. Add only enough water to cover the cut end of the vegetables. The tops must always be above water level.

If cuttings are taken from all three of these vegetables, the rooting bowl will shortly become an attractive arrangement of pale-green fern-like carrot foliage, maroon-red beet leaves, and typical green turnip leafage.

Peanuts

Of all the "for fun plants," my family has enjoyed the rapid-growing peanut the most. It is classified as a Brazilian herbaceous vine with the Latin designation *Arachis hypogaea* and surprisingly is a member of the pea family. Don't miss the fun you will have growing this plant. It will reward you tenfold, will amaze your guests, and will be a constant attraction in your home.

The most difficult part of growing a peanut plant may be obtaining a nonroasted peanut still in its shell. Some seed catalogs do offer them. The fresh unroasted peanut should be removed from its shell and red covering and placed on a moist folded facial tissue and put in a largemouth jar. The top of the jar is then replaced, and the jar is put in an area offering bright light but not full sun. Occasionally it may be necessary to add a half teaspoon of water to keep the tissue moist during this period of germination. When sprouting is evident, transfer the plant to a three-inch pot using any commercial all-purpose house-plant potting soil or garden topsoil. After potting, place your peanut seedling in full sun and keep its soil moist.

Sweet Potato

An attractive trailing vine of the morning-glory family can be easily grown from a sweet potato. Simply take a firm sweet potato, stick toothpicks around the middle, and insert it in a wide-mouth jar or tumbler filled with water. Place the container in a partially shaded location until the emergence of roots. This usually takes a week or two, as it is a slow rooter. Add water when necessary to keep the base of the potato constantly underwater.

When you see substantial growth, move the container to a brighter location. This vine is a fast, vigorous grower that can be trained to cling to a support or left to trail.

Palm

(Phoenix)

One of the most popular palms for the home is the *Phoenix roebelenii*, commonly called the pygmy date. This miniature palm, with its typical fronds, is most attractive and ideal for a small room. The average pygmy date attains a height of approximately three feet. The plant is native to Africa and Asia.

The culture requirements are essentially the same for all palms. The pygmy date does best in partial sun or bright light but not full sun. It will thrive with a day temperature up to 75° F. and a night temperature as low as 55° F. When it is in its active stage, usually between April and October, it requires a constantly moist soil. During the plant's dormant period watering must be drastically reduced. An ideal potting mixture for the palm is common garden topsoil plus equal amounts of peat moss and sand with a small amount of dry manure. Of course, any enriched all-purpose potting mix is equally satisfactory. A monthly application of any all-purpose houseplant fertilizer is sufficient, but all nutrients must be withheld during dormancy. Palms enjoy being pot-bound and thrive with daily room ventilation and periodic foliage cleansing. The pygmy date is pleasingly enemy-free. Propagation may be accomplished by seed, but the chore is definitely not for the weekend gardener.

Philodendron

(Philodendron oxycardium)

This plant, a member of the arum family, has been and still is one of the most popular of all indoor plants. Dozens of philodendron species are available, and one can find small pot or basket-planter types that are ideal for end tables, bookcases, and room-divider shelves. In contrast, tree-size plants, often seen in the lobbies of buildings, can be obtained in tubs.

P. oxycardium, the best-known species, is the one regularly offered for sale in supermarkets. Shiny heart-shaped leaves of sweet-pepper-green are characteristic of this plant.

The popularity of the philodendron is largely due to its gratifying flexibility, which makes it one of the easiest of all houseplants to grow. It will do well with little or no sun. It will even grow in a remote corner offering little more than the low-intensity light of a north or west exposure. The philodendron thrives in a day temperature as high as 75° F. and enjoys a night temperature as low as 55° F. It does best when its soil is kept moist, and it will profit by periodic sink soakings followed by drying-out periods of two to six days. The first signs of overwatering are a change of leaf color and leaf dropping. If the plant is allowed to trail, it will appreciate periodic misting or spraying. This little stalwart will grow equally well in common garden topsoil or in any all-purpose commercial houseplant soil mix. It will do well without supplemental nutrients for a long period of time. Any of the all-purpose houseplant fertilizers are recommended once a month to keep your philodendron in tip-top shape. The plant is virtually enemy-free. New plants may be grown by means of cuttings.

Piggyback Plant

(Tolmiea menziesii)

The distinguishing characteristic of this attractive plant is its tooth-like, fuzzy, heart-shaped leaf. Creeping runners bearing clusters of leaflets of delicate pale green seem to ride piggyback on the surface of the darker-green older leaves, thus giving the plant its name. It seldom grows higher than six inches but develops into a bushy beauty. The piggyback, also called the pickaback, is native to the northern forest ranges of the West Coast and a saxifrage family member.

This plant prefers partial sun, and if a room provides good light, it will thrive with no sun at all. It will do best with a day temperature of 70° F. and a night temperature as low as 55° F. Garden topsoil mixed with peat moss is an ideal soil mixture. It will also do well in any commercial all-purpose potting mix. The plant requires a moist soil for proper growth. Monthly applications of any all-purpose house-plant fertilizer will be sufficient to keep this little gem vigorous and healthy. The piggyback is virtually enemy-free. It may be propagated by transplanting plantlets.

Prayer Plant

(Maranta leuconeura kerchoviana)

The prayer plant is as fascinating as it is attractive, and no collection should be without this little conversation piece. Pale-green velvety foliage with rows of darker-green and brownish patches distinguishes this plant. The unique characteristic of the prayer plant is that at the end of each day the plant's leaves extend upward in the manner of clasped hands in prayer and remain this way all night. At the advent of daybreak the plant's leaves drop from their perpendicular night position until they are once again horizontal. The prayer plant may grow to fifteen inches, and its leaves usually measure six inches. It is native to the tropics and a member of the family Marantaceae.

An east or a west exposure is ideal, because this plant prefers partial shade and definitely does not like full sun. It enjoys a day temperature as high as 75° F. and a night temperature as low as 60° F. Its soil should be kept constantly moist except during dormancy, which begins in the fall. After that, watering should be only sparing and infrequent until January. The prayer plant thrives in high humidity, and foliage misting is most beneficial.

Any all-purpose commercial houseplant soil mix or fortified garden topsoil can be used to grow this interesting ornamental. A high nutritional level can be maintained with an application of any of the all-purpose houseplant fertilizers twice a month, except during the fall dormant period. Propagation can be accomplished by plant division. The prayer plant is easily grown and virtually enemy-free.

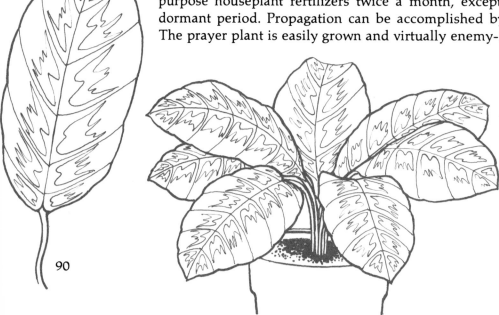

90

Spider Plant

(Chlorophytum elatum)

This is truly a fun plant. It is easy to grow, it is a prolific producer, and best of all the spider plant is unusually tolerant of unfavorable environmental conditions. A decorative foliage plant with long, grass-like, narrow leaves, the *C. elatum* is the most commonly seen species and is recognized by its lustrous green foliage. This plant is at its best when grown in a hanging basket or placed on a shelf above eye level.

The fun this plant affords is associated with its extraordinary ease of propagation that it derives from its proliferous nature. All one needs to do to start a new plant is to place one of the plantlets, still on its runner, in the topsoil of a nearby plant just deep enough to hold it firmly in place. When the plantlet shows appreciable growth, it is then snipped off its runner and allowed to exist as a new plant on its own. Other methods of propagation are accomplished easily by cutting the infant plant from its runner and planting it root side down in a three-inch pot, or one may place a baby plant in a shallow container of water and allow it to remain there until the plant develops a strong root system, after which it is placed in a pot of its own.

This nondemanding plant is most flexible, and its simple culture requirements are as follows: It does equally well in partial sun as in full sun; it enjoys a day temperature as high as 75° F. and a night temperature as low as 50° F.; it is a water-lover, requiring more than most plants; it thrives in any all-purpose commercial potting soil and does well in common garden topsoil; it asks for only an occasional application of any all-purpose houseplant fertilizer.

The spider is native to South Africa and is a member of the lily family. It is comparatively pest-free. An old-time plant, it was enjoyed as much by our grandmothers as it is by modern houseplant-lovers. One full-grown plant will provide you with enough plantlets to expand your own collection and to provide gifts for friends.

Strawberry Geranium, or Strawberry Begonia

(Saxifraga sarmentosa)

This little gem is misleadingly named, for it is not a begonia species nor a member of the geranium family. Rather, it is a member of the saxifrage family. One explanation of its name is that it produces strawberrylike runners and has leaves that are similar to the geranium's. It is a trailing-type plant that is at its best when grown in a hanging basket. Its reddish leaves are veined in white, and their edges are scalloped. Its manner of reproduction is a distinguishing characteristic. At first, runners appear, and eventually a group of minute leaflets bursts out of the tip of each runner. A mature strawberry begonia will grow best in a three- to five-inch pot. The plant is native to Asia.

It prefers sunlight but will do well in a room with little sun providing there is bright light. A day temperature as high as 75° F. and a night temperature as low as 55° F. are ideal. Its soil should be kept on the moist side, and it will grow properly in any commercial all-purpose potting-soil mix or in common garden topsoil. An application of any all-purpose houseplant fertilizer once a month will be sufficient. If this plant is attacked, the responsible culprit will usually be the mealybug. Propagation may be accomplished by means of runners.

Velvet Plant

(Gynura aurantiaca)

G. aurantiaca is an attractive foliage plant that has brilliant, luminous, purplish leaves with a furry surface giving the plant a smoky or satin appearance. Unlike many hairy- or fuzzy-surfaced plants, the leaves of this plant are as pleasing to touch as luxurious velvet.

The velvet plant is a member of the composite family. It is native to Java and is usually classified as a medium to low plant. If allowed to grow without pruning, however, it can grow to a height of thirty inches and become an unattractive straggler.

The velvet is a sun plant, and a southern exposure is to its liking. It will tolerate a day temperature as high as 75° F. and a night temperature as low as 65° F. This plant requires an environment of high humidity, which can be maintained by daily foliage misting. Its soil should be kept moist, and it will grow properly in fortified common garden topsoil or in any commercial all-purpose houseplant soil mix. Liquid manure or an application of any all-purpose houseplant fertilizer twice a month is recommended. The velvet plant is pest-free. It is easily propagated by cuttings.

Wandering Jew

(Zebrina pendula) (Tradescantia fluminensis)

The designation "wandering Jew" is commonly applied to two related species, *Z. pendula* and *T. fluminensis.* Both are members of the spiderwort family. These fast-growing, trailing-type plants are most attractive when grown in hanging baskets. Ideal for the novice, these plants are virtually care-free and most flexible.

These species of zebrina and tradescantia will grow equally well in full sun or partial shade. They enjoy a day temperature as high as 75° F. and a night temperature as low as 55° F. Their soil, which should be kept uniformly moist, may be a mixture of common garden topsoil or any all-purpose commercial potting-soil mix. Either species will reward its owner with vigorous growth if given an application of any all-purpose potted-plant fertilizer once a month. These plants are usually enemy-free and may be propagated easily by means of cuttings.

The *Z. pendula,* a native of Mexico, is widely favored for its silver-striped, translucent, reddish-purple foliage.

The *T. fluminensis* has a more oval-shaped leaf with an underside of colorful magenta and is a native of South America.

Succulent Plants

Succulent plants have the inherent ability to store water within their leaves and stems, which enables them to exist for reasonably long periods without water. Cacti are succulents, but all succulents are not cacti. Regardless of this botanical distinction, the culture requirements of both succulents and cacti are, for all practical purposes, the same. (The designation "cactus" is of Greek derivation, from *kaktos,* adopted and applied by the renowned Swedish botanist Carolus Linnaeus [1707–1778], and is now considered to include all members of the enormous family Cactaceae.)

Most succulents do best in full sun and especially bright light. They even thrive under fluorescent lighting. They enjoy a day temperature below 75° F., with a night temperature as low as 55° F. These plants will do well with rich garden topsoil modified by the addition of builder's sand, grit, gravel, or small pieces of broken clay pots, plus bone meal and limestone. Most indoor gardeners will find it more convenient to use any of the special commercial cactus mixes. Good drainage is essential. Most succulents require watering only once or twice a month, with their soil kept dry during the interim. Daily ventilation is beneficial. These plants enjoy being planted in small-sized pots. Succulents are easily managed and virtually pest-free. The rare case of infestation will usually be due to the mealybug or the red spider. Succulents are very popular when arranged, as a collection, in a deep tray or as a dish garden.

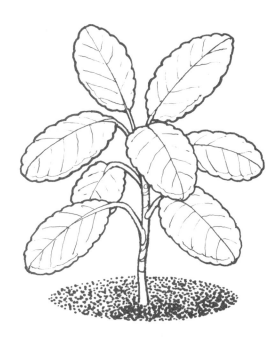

Air Plant, or Life Plant

(Bryophyllum pinnatum)

This succulent is not only a fun plant but also one that quickly becomes a conversation piece. It will grow equally well in full sun or partial sunlight. The plant is native to the tropics and a member of the figwort family. The unique manner in which it may be propagated is a distinguishing characteristic. One needs only to remove a leaf of the plant and pin it to a drape or curtain, and in a very short time plantlets will emerge from each of the leaf's scalloped edges. Eventually, these new plantlets can be removed from their mother leaf and potted.

Ball Cactus

(Notocactus)

This is an interesting group of globular-shaped cacti that are native to South America. They bear a single two-inch flower that appears from the side of the plant's domed top in the same manner and angle that a maiden would wear a flower in her hair. There are several species of this plant, but in general they differ only as to height, width, and type of surface.

97

Bishop's-Hood Cactus

(Astrophytum myriostigma)

This is an attractive spineless low-growing cactus plant, usually two to three inches high, whose dome is divided into five sections, similar to the liturgical headdress, or miter, worn by bishops. This plant bears a single buttercup-yellow flower on the top of its dome.

Christmas Cactus

(Schlumbergera bridgesii)

A holiday-season charmer, the scalloped or segmented, glossy, waxy green branches of the Christmas cactus are flat, and each segment is usually one to two inches long. With proper culture this plant will produce a brilliant display of gorgeous multipetaled cherry-red flowers that dangle on the end of the plant's pendulous, segmented branches. These holiday blossoms can be as long as three inches. Propagation can be accomplished by cuttings or seeds. About the end of October or the first of November, a program of twelve to fourteen hours of absolute darkness each day for thirty days is necessary to stimulate bud formation and to assure handsome blooms during the holiday season.

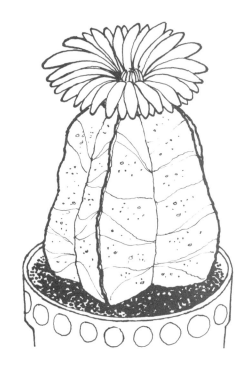

Jade Plant

(Crassula argentea)

This popular dwarf, treelike succulent is recognized by its heavy trunk and fleshy, waxy green leaves. If left on its own without pruning, it can attain a height of five feet. The jade likes full sun. This is an interesting, easily grown plant, which is propagated by terminal stem or leaf cuttings. It is native to Africa and a member of the orpine family.

Old-Man Cactus

(Cephalocereus senilis)

This cactus is a curious South American obelisk-shaped plant that is distinguished by long, hairlike strands that dangle from the plant's pointed top. With proper culture the plant will produce dusty-pink flowers, which emerge from the white hair of the "old man."

Pincushion Cactus

(Mammillaria)

Having species that bear white, yellow, cream, or red flowers, most of these desert-type plants are spherical in shape, and their tops resemble the old-fashioned pincushion. Their surfaces are evenly covered with red, gray, white, or black spines. Propagation is by lateral offshoots.

Grafted Cacti and Succulents for Dish Gardens

The following excerpts are reprinted by permission of the George W. Park Seed Company.

Everyone should have a hobby . . . cacti. Only one who has seen the desert in bloom can believe the beauty that crowns these unusual plants.

Interesting, easy to care for, and often exotically beautiful, these plants are well adapted for pot culture. As a houseplant, they are ideal because of their ability to thrive with minimum care.

CACTUS BUNNIES. These coiffured cuties stand just three inches tall, eye-catching specimens with medium-green lightly spined stalks topped by bright heads about an inch across, delicately fluted, corrugated, and spined. Just imagine these colorful plants in a dish garden.

HIPPIE. Long hair is the style of the day, even in cactus. *Espostoa lanata* grafted on *Triangularis* is a real freak. Unusual by itself and excellent in a dish garden.

CREW CUT. Gives that needed note of conservatism to your dish garden. Cute and cheerful, its spines resemble a fresh haircut. A nice addition to a collection.

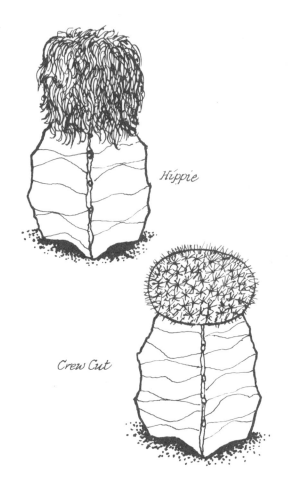

Hippie

Crew Cut

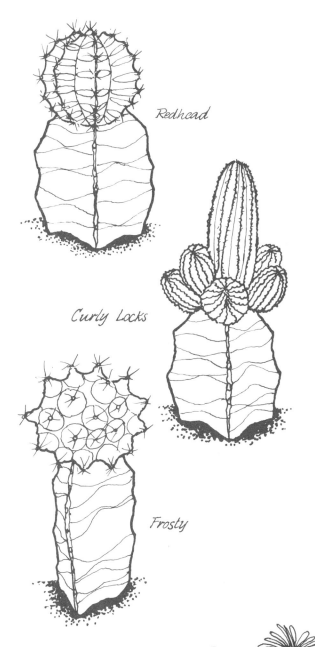

Redhead

Curly Locks

Frosty

GIBSON GIRL. Grafted atop *Triangularis* are clusters of *Notocactus* making for an unusual attraction. The bright-green stalk is topped by bronze clusters.

REDHEAD. Bright-scarlet crown grafted on *Triangularis*. Exceptionally colorful.

CURLY LOCKS. Pale lime-colored heads are elongated and irregular in formation. Very unique atop *Triangularis* stalks.

BLONDIE. Golden-yellow *Gymnocalycium* head grafted atop deep-green *Triangularis* stalk. Interesting alone, fascinating with others.

FROSTY. White with a hint of pink.

SUCCULENTS FOR DISH GARDENS. Living Stones, Mimicry mixed. Highly curious collection of succulents. Flowers appear September, and their strong colors contrast effectively with the silvery or bluish stems. *Echeveria*, succulent leaf rosettes of various pastel colors with small flowers of red, pink, or yellow, usually in spikes. They are grown indoors in pots and dish arrangements and sometimes bedded out in summer.

Living Stones

Appendixes

I keep six honest serving-men
(They taught me all I knew);
Their names are What and Why and When
And How and Where and Who.

—Rudyard Kipling

Books for the Indoor Gardener

All about Begonias, Bernice Brilmayer. New York: Doubleday, 1960.

All about Miniature Plants and Gardens, Bernice Brilmayer. New York: Doubleday, 1963.

All about Vines and Hanging Plants, Bernice Brilmayer. New York: Doubleday, 1962.

Begonias, Indoors and Out, Jack Kramer. New York: Dutton, 1967.

The Book of Cacti and Other Succulents, Claude Chidamian. New York: Doubleday, 1958.

Bromeliads, the Colorful House Plants, Jack Kramer. Princeton, N.J.: Van Nostrand, 1965.

Cacti for the Amateur, Scott E. Haselton. Pasadena, Calif.: Abbey Garden Press, 1958.

The City Gardener, Philip Truex. New York: Knopf, 1964.

Flowering Bulbs for Winter Windows, Marion C. Walker. Princeton, N.J.: Van Nostrand, 1965.

Fluorescent Light Gardening, Elaine C. Cherry. Princeton, N.J.: Van Nostrand, 1965.

Foliage Plants for Indoor Gardening, James Underwood Crockett. New York: Doubleday, 1967.

The Gardener's Fern Book, Gordon Foster. Princeton, N.J.: Van Nostrand, 1964.

Greenhouse Gardening as a Hobby, James Underwood Crockett. New York: Doubleday, 1961.

Growing Orchids at Your Windows, Jack Kramer. Princeton, N.J.: Van Nostrand, 1963.

The Joy of Geraniums, Helen Van Pelt Wilson. New York: Barrows, 1967.

Miniature Plants for Home and Greenhouse, Elvin McDonald. Princeton, N.J.: Van Nostrand, 1963.

The Miniature Rose Book, Margaret E. Pinney. Princeton, N.J.: Van Nostrand, 1964.

The New Complete Book of African-Violets, Helen Van Pelt Wilson. New York: Barrows, 1963.

1000 Beautiful House Plants and How to Grow Them, Jack Kramer. New York: William Morrow, 1969.

1001 House Plant Questions Answered, Stanley Schuler. Princeton, N.J.: Van Nostrand, 1963.

Variegated Foliage Plants, Paul Fischer. London: Blandford Press, 1960.

Periodicals and Societies for the Indoor Gardener

African Violet Society of America
P.O. Box 1326
Knoxville, Tennessee 37901
African Violet Magazine

American Begonia Society
1510 Kimberly Avenue
Anaheim, California 92802
The Begonian

American Camellia Society
P.O. Box C
Tifton, Georgia 31794
American Camellia Journal

American Fern Society
415 South Pleasant Street
Amherst, Massachusetts 01002
American Fern Journal

American Gloxinian Society
Eastford, Connecticut 06242
The Gloxinian and the Other Gesneriads

American Hibiscus Society
P.O. Box 98
Eagle Lake, Florida 33839
The Seed Pod

American Orchid Society
Botanical Museum of Harvard University
Cambridge, Massachusetts 02138
American Orchid Society Bulletin

American Plant Life Society
Box 150
La Jolla, California 92037
Plant Life

American Poinsettia Society
Box 94
Mission, Texas 78572
Bulletin

The Bromeliad Society
1811 Edgecliff Drive
Los Angeles, California 90026
Bromeliad Society Bulletin

Cactus and Succulent Journal
132 West Union Street
Pasadena, California 91101

California National Fuchsia Society
6124 South Rimbank Avenue
Pico Rivera, California 90660
The National Fuchsia Fan

Epiphyllum Society of America
4400 Portola Avenue
Los Angeles, California 90032
Bulletin

Greater New York Orchid Society
338 East 83rd Street
New York, New York 10028
Orchidata

International Geranium Society
1413 Bluff Drive
Santa Barbara, California 93105
Geraniums around the World

National Chrysanthemum Society Bulletin
345 Milton Road
Rye, New York 10580

Saintpaulia International
P.O. Box 10604
Knoxville, Tennessee 37919
Gesneriad-Saintpaulia News

Where to Order Plants, Bulbs, Seeds, and Supplies

The courteous indoor gardener always encloses a first-class stamp when sending for a free catalog and makes certain that he has included his full name and address, including zip code, and the correct amount of change when there is a charge.

ALBERTS & MERKEL BROS., 2210 South Federal Highway, Boynton Beach, Florida 33435. Orchids and tropical foliage plants. Catalog $1.00.

ARTHUR EAMES ALLGROVE, North Wilmington, Massachusetts 01887. Ferns, terrarium plants, bonsai, saikei, and wild flowers. Catalog 50¢.

ARMSTRONG ASSOCIATES, INC., Box 127, Basking Ridge, New Jersey 07920. Carnivorous plants of all types and terrarium plants. Catalog 25¢.

BEAHM GARDENS, 2686 Paloma Street, Pasadena, California 91107. Epiphyllums, hoyas, rhipsalis. Catalog free.

BIDDLE SERVICE, Hawthorne, New York 10532. Supplies and equipment for flowers and plants. Catalog 10¢.

BOYCAN'S CRAFT SUPPLIES, 1052 East State Street, Sharon, Pennsylvania 16146. Flower accessories, such as holders and pots, plus artificial-flower-making materials. Catalog 50¢.

BUELL'S GREENHOUSES, P.O. Box 218, Eastford, Connecticut 06242. African violets, gloxinias, soil, pots, supplies. Catalog 25¢, plus stamped (16¢) self-addressed long envelope.

BURGESS SEED AND PLANT CO., 67 East Battle Creek Street, Galesburg, Michigan 49053. Full line of seeds, plants, and nursery stock. Catalog free.

CALIFORNIA JUNGLE GARDENS, 11977 San Vincente Boulevard, Los Angeles, California 90049. Miscellany of interesting tropical plants, including fifty kinds of ferns. Catalog 25¢.

COOK'S GERANIUM NURSERY, 712 North Grand, Lyons, Kansas 67554. Geraniums, zonals, scented leaf, fancy leaf, ivy leaf, odd, unusual, and rare. Catalog 25¢.

C. A. CRUICKSHANK, LTD., 1015 Mount Pleasant Road, Toronto M4P2M1, Ontario, Canada. Bulbs, seeds, plant stands, miniature greenhouses, fluorescent fixtures. Catalog free.

L. EASTERBROOK GREENHOUSES, 10 Craig Street, Butler, Ohio 44822. African violets, gesneriads, begonias, ferns, terrarium plants. Catalog 50¢ and 25¢, depending on size.

FARMER SEED & NURSERY CO., Fairbault, Minnesota 55021. Full line of nursery plants including midgets, bred primarily for northern tier states and the prairie provinces of Canada. Catalog free.

FENNELL ORCHID CO., 26715 S.W. 157th Avenue, Homestead, Florida 33030. Live orchid plants and orchid supplies. Catalog 25¢.

FISCHER GREENHOUSES, Oak Avenue, Linwood, New Jersey 08211. African violets, gesneriads, and supplies. Catalog 15¢, supply list 20¢.

FLORALITE COMPANY, 4124 East Oakwood Road, Oak Creek, Wisconsin 53154. Indoor-gardening supplies, plant stands, fluorescent fixtures, full line Vita-Lite, Plant-Lite, and Gro-Lux tubes. Catalog 8¢ stamp.

FRENCH'S BULB IMPORTER, P.O. Box 87, Center Rutland, Vermont 05736. Spring-flowering bulbs, forcing bulbs, and seed for greenhouse use. Catalog 25¢.

JOSEPH HARRIS CO., INC., 3670 Buffalo Road, Rochester, New York 14624. Seeds, garden supplies. Catalog free.

HORTICULTURAL SUPPLIES, 3548 North Cramer Street, Milwaukee, Wisconsin 53211. Complete line of growing supplies for African violet indoor gardeners. Catalog 25¢.

HOUSE PLANT CORNER, 100 West Division Street, Box 810, Oxford, Maryland 21654. Supplies, fluorescent-light equipment. Catalog 25¢.

HYDROPONIC CHEMICAL CO., INC., Box 4300, Copley, Ohio 44321. HYPONeX Plant Foods and other products. Catalog free.

P. D. JAGER & SONS, INC., 188 Asbury Street, South Hamilton, Massachusetts 01982. Flower bulbs. Catalog free.

KARTUZ GREENHOUSES, 92 Chestnut Street, Wilmington, Massachusetts 01887. Gesneriads, begonias, miniatures, dwarf geraniums, succulents, supplies. Catalog 50¢.

KELLY BROS. NURSERY, INC., 23 Maple Street, Dansville, New York 14477. Complete line of nursery plants. Catalog free.

LOGEE'S GREENHOUSES, 55 North Street, Danielson, Connecticut 06239. Over eighteen hundred named varieties of indoor plants; also the rare and the unusual. Catalog $1.00.

LYNDON LYON, 14 Mutchler Street, Dolgeville, New York 13329. African violets, gesneriads, and other houseplants. Catalog free.

MERRY GARDENS, P.O. Box 595, Camden, Maine 04843. Rare indoor plants and greenhouse plants. Catalog, picture handbook $1.00, list 25¢.

GEO. W. PARK SEED CO., Greenwood, South Carolina 29646. Flower and vegetable seeds and growing supplies. Catalog available.

SHOPLITE CO., 650 Franklin Avenue, Nutley, New Jersey 07110. Fluorescent-light equipment, stands, fixtures, full line of growth bulbs. Catalog 25¢.

TERRESTRIS GREENHOUSES, INC., 409 East 60th Street, New York, New York 10022. Tropical indoor plants. Catalog $1.00 by mail, free at greenhouse.

TINARI GREENHOUSES, 2325 Valley Road, Huntingdon Valley, Pennsylvania 19006. African violets, related supplies, lighting equipment. Catalog 25¢.

TUBE CRAFT, INC., 1311 West 80th Street, Cleveland, Ohio 44102. Flora Cart and accessories. Catalog upon request.

WILSON BROTHERS FLORAL COMPANY, INC., Roachdale, Indiana 46172. Geraniums, African violets, and novelty houseplants. Catalog free.